COMFORT MY PEOPLE

COMFORT MY PEOPLE

Comfort, comfort my people,
says your God . . .
*   —Isaiah 40:1, 13*

Comfort My People

The Pastoral Presence of the Church

by EUGENE C. KENNEDY, M.M.

SHEED AND WARD: *New York*

The author wishes to thank the editors of *The Critic* for permission to reprint two chapters which first appeared in their pages.

Contents

Introduction

The world is trying to tell us something. It does this in a confused mixture of styles, sometimes through the echoless silence of its alienation and at other times in the furious, multi-colored whirlwind of its wars and entertainments. Behind all of this man is a hunter, stalking himself, seeking his own meaning in a trembling universe. The world is saying that it seeks something of lasting value, something that will help it to find itself and give it truths by which it can live genuinely. Men are saying, whether they recognize it or not, that they need the words of eternal life spoken by a Church that genuinely understands them and their longing for life to the full.

Gregory Baum has pointed out that in the documents of Vatican II the term *Church* has several meanings. It can refer to the Church as the Roman Catholic Church, composed of those who explicitly acknowledge the hierarchical ministry and celebrate the seven sacramental actions of Christ. It can also refer to the local congregation, to Christ in the presence of those who stand around the altar together. Beyond these, Church also designates the community of all the baptized, and also the "Church universal" as it pertains to all mankind summoned and transformed by divine Grace. Church also designates the mystery of relationship in the Spirit of those who are friends or who are becoming friends, in contrast to men in conflict with themselves and separated by alienation from others.

It is in this latter sense especially that I speak of the Church in this book. This is the open Church which presents itself as the People of God in the caravans of whose pilgrimage there is room for all. It is the Church of those called to be friends and to share the life of the Spirit with each other. This is the Church whose pastoral presence is so desperately looked for by men today. It is the community of believers who gather, not to hide in the hills in anticipation of some prophet's doomsday, but to give life to each other through the love that arises from the action of the Holy Spirit. This is indeed the Church which can understand man and his agonies, which can bind up his wounds, and offer him redemption through its invitation to life in and through the community of Christ. This is the Church that comes into being whenever men truly open themselves in faith and hope to one another.

I have written this book to reflect on the basic Christian attitude of defenseless service to others. An individual does not find faith out of the blue. In the human process, a man will not believe "unless someone shows" him (Acts 8:31). Faith comes through hearing, through personal interaction, through incarnation, death, and resurrection in relationship to other persons. The incarnational vocation of the Church bids all Churchmen and Churchwomen to share in making the pastoral presence of the saving mystery come truly to life in the family of man.

In the document on "The Church in the Modern World," the council Fathers ask—

What does the Church think of man? . . . People are waiting for an answer. From the answers it will be increasingly clear that the People of God and the human race in whose midst it lives render service to each other. Thus the mission of the Church will show its religious, and by that very fact, its supremely human character.[1]

The Church cannot be religious unless it is fully human. There has been a long and trying tendency on the part of some spiritual commentators to be suspicious of this basic truth. This has led to an indictment of human relationships as not being supernatural, as though the mystery of salvation were to be accomplished between disembodied spirits rather than persons. But the setting of redemption is the world, not the desert retreats that reject it. Men live the life of the Spirit in community with one another, not in breathless strivings to escape one another. The great message that the deeply human Church has for all men lies in offering them a community that calls them out of their suffocating and self-defeating isolation from each other. The Church's mission is to bring men into true community with each other under the action of the Spirit. This cannot and will not occur unless the Church is fully committed to its incarnate vocation. It is when the Church forgets or misunderstands its humanity that it fails to understand its relevance to the world.

The basic attitude of the Church can only be manifested in the open human attitudes of its members. Here is where the Spirit breathes on men and brings them to life. The most important instrumentality of the Church is its human personality. This does not exist aside from the human personalities of its members. The essays in this book will, I hope, help the Church's servants to understand and accept their own humanity, to forgive themselves for it, and to assist them in giving the full gift of it to others. The more truly human they are the more fully can they be the agents of the Spirit in the work of redemption. I am afraid that too many of the Church's servants have been trained not to trust or value their own humanity. This has led to a great deal of non-redemptive suffering in their lives and has prevented them from being as free and loving as God's servants have a right to be.

It continues to amaze me to notice the sense of relief that many of the Church's servants experience when they realize that they are not called to be angels and that it is all right for them to be human beings. Once they can admit themselves into the human race and accept their necessary imperfection they find the freedom of God's children and can give themselves in genuine service to others. That is really what life is all about. It is what the life of the Spirit is all about as well.

What else do we have to give to others except ourselves a little more unselfishly each day? Buildings and blueprints will mock us eternally if we do not understand the Church as a mystery that fundamentally transcends them. The persons who are God's people are the only prize in the apostolate. What else is there in life for a servant of the Church than his people? How else can the Church be made present if we fail, in the real meaning of the poverty of the apostles, to give our imperfect persons unreservedly and unconditionally for the sake of others? Salvation is a human enterprise. It is for men. It comes through men who are ready to love other men, not for their praise or even for credits in the ledgers of heaven. We are called to love other men, not because we conjure up Christ in them, but because they are men and they need us. That is why Christ loved them and gave himself up for them.

This is a perilous task, this invitation to become relevant through our relationships with other men. It is the kind of activity that can hurt and even destroy us. Several months ago, in an incredible accident in Vietnam, a live grenade was lodged in the back of a civilian. Careful preparations were made for this delicate surgery. Walls of sandbags and shatterproof glass were erected. The doctor was protectively dressed and provided with an extended instrument to perform the operation on this man, so cruelly a victim and a threat at the same time. Whenever we minister, with some sense of Christian love to men wounded by life or sin, we can all too easily approach them with the same caution.

But men are suffering and dying and crying for help. We can be overwhelmed by the sense of threat that arises if we place ourselves at their side. It is not good enough to reach out to man from behind sandbags that make us secure, from behind shatterproof glass that saves ourselves. The world has a right to something better than that from us, from men and women whose love exposes them to pain and hurt in saving others.

Our persons must be involved if we seriously take on the responsibilities of the pastoral presence of the Church. We have lots of sandbags and shatterproof glass, all fashioned in the age of clerical culture that made us focus excessively on our own perfection, sometimes at the price of failing to give ourselves to the service of the Church. I do not think the sandbags give us much protection anymore, and, as we should have known all along, people can see through glass, even if it is shatterproof.

The servants of the People of God find themselves exposed to all the dangers of relevancy. For them the post-conciliar milieu is one of tension, the invigorating tension that arises because their own persons are so intimately and completely engaged in the work of redeeming their brothers. This book is not aimed at dissolving the healthy tension of life in the Spirit. Hopefully, it will help some to recognize and accept this tension as a sign that they not only have life but that they can hand it on, even though they are imperfect, to others.

The reader will notice that I use the terms priest, pastor, and pastoral figure somewhat interchangeably throughout these essays. This is because the pastoral work of the Church, particularly in this time of evolving apostolates, is a responsibility which the priest shares with religious brothers and sisters and laymen. The priest may be the central figure in the pastoral presence of the Church but he is not isolated or insulated from others in the role. What I have written can be applied to all Christians who participate in making the Church a living presence in the world.

I have really written only an introductory series of reflections on this subject, prompted by my experience with the churchmen and churchwomen, clergy, religious, and laity alike, who have, through their own persons, given me an experience of the Church. I hope in some way to have captured the glints of the Spirit that make them the light of the world. If there is truth in any of my words, it is because these genuine Christians have made the words of life flesh through their own persons, and have shared themselves freely and generously with me.

Eugene C. Kennedy, M.M.

Glen Ellyn, Illinois
March 13, 1968
F.S.

Notes

1. *The Documents of Vatican II*, ed. by Walter M. Abbott, S.J. (New York: Guild Press, America Press, and Association Press, 1966), pp. 209–210.

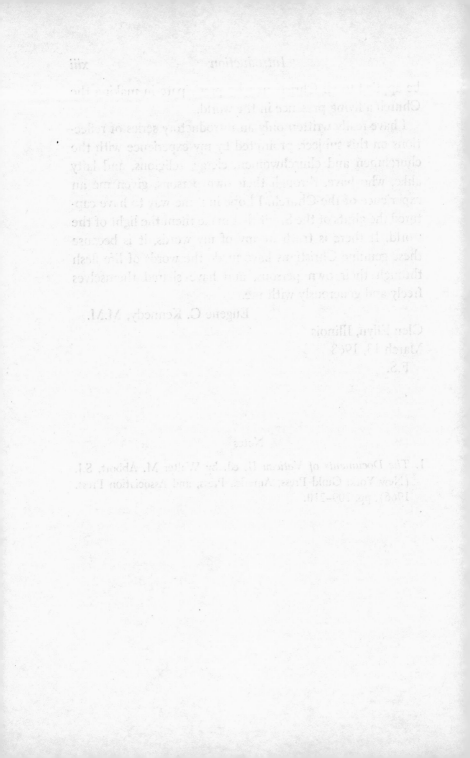

1

The Dissolution of Clerical Culture

At this tenuous moment in Salvation History any discussion of pastoral psychology must begin with those persons who are called by the Holy Spirit to serve the People of God as pastors. The ministers of the Church are caught in the great rolling wave of renewal and are being washed ashore on new and uncharted shorelines. Everywhere priests are bobbing about in the tides, looking for friendly lights and saving rescue lines. Feeling washed overboard from their secure stations on the ship of Peter, some wonder if they were ever meant to be seamen in the first place.

They cannot walk the waters and Christ does not calm the storm for them. They are swimming, some for the first time unassisted, and this is a good thing. It is healthy because they are struggling against forces that had not previously challenged them. The questions that fill their minds as they slog ashore range from "How did I get into this life?" to "How do I get out of it?" The priests of the Church wonder about their identity and function and the answers do not come easily. The important point is that they are actively struggling with these basic problems and that they

1

are tapping unsuspected strengths of their own in the process. As long as this is true they are not quite as lost as they
may seem in this unfamiliar and uncomforting new environment.

The present crisis for priests finds them unsure of themselves but they are at least vitally engaged in trying to understand their identity and their work of ministry. They have
been forced to look into themselves and at the style of their
life. This is not unlike the experience of the Protestant ministry earlier in this century. It is, of course, an extremely
threatening experience because, shorn of formerly clearly
defined functions, they must dig into their own personal
resources to respond to the situation. They can no longer
depend on an organizational structure of Catholicism to
tell them exactly who they are and what they are expected
to do in the service of the organization. Their own persons
are exposed as they never have been before and while this is
distinctly uncomfortable, it is also exhilarating.

Much of what is happening to them is not well understood. They tend, in fact, to think that the epic transformation of the Church means the disintegration of the
priesthood itself. Thus there are those who question the very
existence of a non-episcopal priesthood. "Could not a lay
person do what I do, and in many cases do it better?" is a
hauntingly familiar current question. Others respond by
trying to reaffirm or reinforce a former structure of priestly
life. "When will things get back to normal?" they ask, and
the answer, of course, is "Never." What is occurring is not,
in my opinion, the disintegration of the priesthood as much
as the disintegration of a form of clerical culture which had

been dangerously overidentified with the priesthood itself.

This requires explanation. In the United States a whole pattern of priestly life is being reorganized. This is an extremely confusing phenomenon, especially for those who are experiencing it, but not a disastrous one. It was, in fact, predictable and it is, in essence, hopeful. The life-style for priests in America developed along with Catholicism and it is being transformed as American Catholicism is transformed.

The traditions of priestly life in the New World have always placed the priest in an important and at times dominant relationship with his people. He was a leader, a shepherd to an underprivileged flock anxious to maintain and protect its faith in a new-found land. The priest was for a long time the best educated person in the Christian community, the majority of whose members were just getting a handhold on the lowest rung of the social and economic ladders. The priest was a figure of authority to whom peoples accustomed to European authoritarian environments both instinctively and necessarily turned for guidance and support. Indeed, American priests fought many battles for the basic civil rights of their people. Long before Selma they doggedly marched and protested for the dignity of their struggling immigrant flocks. Beyond that they interacted with them in a whole range of needs from settling strikes to helping them fill out their citizenship papers. It is a rich tradition, the American priest and the American Catholic people, a relationship far closer than that of priest and people in Europe.

The early American priest won the respect that was given

to him. The hats that are tipped to us today are a salute to these long dead clergymen. The priest enjoyed prestige and power in the rather closed Catholic ethnic communities that constituted the patchwork entity of the American Church. The Catholic family that could give a son (or daughter) to the Church enjoyed a satisfying mixture of pride and achievement. The son and daughter so given generally improved their status as they moved into the pleasantly warm limelight of Catholic approval and admiration. The Catholic culture was somewhat self-contained within the American landscape and it gladly gave reverence and privilege to its highly prized clerical sons and religious daughters.

This closed quality of the Catholic world in the United States may seem, from our perspective, to have placed the clergy on a pedestal with a disdain for reality known only by dreamy idealists. In any case, the end result was the emergence of the priesthood as a profession of great influence and dignity. Priests were respected for their sacrifice and their service and this presented an admirable vocational ideal which proved highly attractive to qualified young men. They did more than fulfill a desire to serve the Church when they entered the ranks of the clergy. They also found one of the few avenues of higher education and cultural development then available to Catholics. They also, whether they were motivated by it or not, entered a system that offered security if not affluence, and the warm affection of the Catholic people. The insular nature of the Catholic presence in America developed a structure which understandably produced a healthy supply of vocations. The priests arose from the Catholic culture that acclaimed them, and went back to it to provide attractive models of the priestly life for other young men to follow.

The life of the priest, like his training, tended to reinforce his separate and chosen character. He was removed from the world, as an uncut diamond from the encrusting earth, underwent a careful course of preparation and polishing, and at last was reinserted in the splendid new setting of clerical life. The development of a priestly class was an inevitable occurrence. The priest was expected to be apart from the Catholic people in many ways. He was unmarried, he was presumed to be a model of holiness, and he was properly of the class that seemed in some way or other to have proprietary rights to the Roman Catholic Church. There are relics of this separated clerical life still extant. The priesthood is referred to as a "league," the defecting priest identified as one who has "jumped the league." The Forty Hours celebrations, once appropriate gatherings for priests who could see each other but seldom, are splendid social affairs whose high spirits would be destroyed by the presence of anyone who didn't wear a Roman collar. A priest was advised to make his friends with his brother priests and to maintain a certain distance or even aloofness from the laity. Great emphasis was put on such things as "class" loyalty so that all the members of the same ordination group looked especially to one another for friendship and support. Vacations and other recreations were taken together and all this was considered appropriate and healthy. The clergy needed this kind of support especially in the less Catholic areas of the country. It is even understandable in the great metropolitan centers where the Catholic enterprise flourished.

There was, after all, a general feeling that the priest was an available and adaptable man, ready to grab his bags and shift from parish to parish in resolute obedience. This was part of the reason that he was so admired. If these changes were a natural part of his clerical life he did need a supportive set of social relationships that transcended parish boundaries and outlasted tours of duty at various rectories. These he found in large measure with his brother priests or with his family. But his family, despite the durability of many Irish and German mothers, gradually changed as the priest grew older. He needed some sense of identity with his comrades and this was achieved within the ranks of the priesthood itself. Indeed, camaraderie persists as a great characteristic of clerical gatherings even to this day.

What I am saying is that for a whole series of reasons, a well-knit clerical culture developed within American Catholicism. It was rewarded by the respect of this larger context even as it was supported by it financially. The priesthood took on many aspects of a caste life and reinforced itself in this position through the nature of seminary training and the conditions of rectory life. The well-behaved cleric belonged to a fraternity of priests and was comfortable among them. He received much personal support in this inner world and moved away from it at his own peril.

The tightness of the Catholic and clerical worlds explains the traditional over-reaction to any young man who left either the seminary or the priesthood. The ex-seminarian had sinned against tribal unity and was eyed ever afterwards somewhat suspiciously as a "spoiled priest," forbidden, often by explicit rule, to write to or to visit the seminary he had left. The priest who left the priesthood had let the team down, was a failure, a defector to some undefinable other world. These examples illustrate the psychological reaction of the group he had left behind. So strong were the bonds of loyalty and unity that anyone who violated them invited a vocabulary of invective to describe his action.

There was, of course, a great deal that was healthy and strong in this Catholic culture. Few countries, even those traditionally Catholic, have seen the working class remain so loyal and generous to the faith. Few clergies can be as justifiably proud of their zeal and accomplishments as the American. The unfortunate but understandable excesses of clericalism diminish but do not destroy this tradition. Clericalism, at its worst, was and is the unthinking capitalization on the positions of trust and privilege accorded to priests. It is the irresponsible attitude that enables some priests and bishops to think of the Church as their own possession and to assume embarrassingly defensive postures in relationship to the laity, as though the latter were Mohammedan hordes bent on the sack of Christendom.

Clericalism is, curiously enough, a disease a man can suffer from and never even realize it. It is that strange infection that blurs a man's vision of reality so that he thinks that rights and privileges, from clerical discounts to getting parking tickets fixed, are irrevocably his merely because he wears a Roman collar. He expects preferential treatment, that everything will be nice for Father, even when he has not earned it by his labors. It is the terrible affliction that

allows a man to perform his duties carelessly and unprofes-
sionally because he is insensitive to the needs and demands
of his people. Clericalism is the exemption from the rules by
which ordinary men must live. Thus the clerical mind can
fail to answer invitations and still show up at the last moment, forget to return phone calls and still be forgiven, fail
to say thank you and still expect to be invited again. It is a
subtle but fatal disease. It is against these and a similar host
of impositions that anti-clerical feelings are directed. Priests
with a larger sense of Christian values have always disowned
the clerical mentality, that frame of mind that so naturally
developed in the Catholic enclave, but the problem has
been widespread nonetheless.

What is happening in our time is the fragmentation of
the Catholic world in the United States and the consequent
crumbling of clerical culture. The Catholics of the United
States are immigrants no longer. Neither are they so defensive about their faith nor restricted in their opportunities
for education and social advancement. They have broken
out of the structure they needed so badly in more oppressive
times. They are as well or better educated than the priest
and they no longer give him automatic adulation and respect. The inner world of the Catholic priesthood, the social
structure of Roman-collared camaraderie, is disintegrating
as these overall changes take place.

The evidence for this is to be found everywhere. The
monastic model of seminary training has faltered because
the priest can no longer be prepared to live a separate and
strangely self-centered kind of life. The possessive attitudes
of the hierarchy which led Bishops to look on the Church

as "theirs" is challenged by a new theology and a deepened grasp by the faithful that they are the People of God. The people are rapidly moving out of the shadow of this once effective authoritarianism into a Christian posture of life marked by greater independence in thought and judgment. Interestingly enough, they are not really interested in fighting the old authoritarianism. They are instead ignoring it.

Authoritarianism ends up howling into the void because the numbers still sensitive to its strictures grow smaller every day. The structure of authoritarianism is no longer effective even in the strictly political realm of Church activity. Offering shelter to no one, it is collapsing. The authoritarian aspect of clerical culture necessarily collapses with it. The mode of relationship between priests and people is in need of radical revision because, while the authoritarian clerical culture crumbles, newer modes of relationship between priests and people have not been supplied.

In fact, this is the source of much of the present stress. The old order is changing in reality but the Church has not yet readjusted itself to this fact in the realm of the life of the priest and the whole range of his dealings with his people. Older priests grew up in the now moribund clerical culture, so its dissolution is destroying the only structures of life that they have ever known. All the familiar rites and practices of the priesthood from hearing confessions to offering Mass have been transformed within a few years. The style of spirituality that nourished them has been repudiated. They have found their prestige and security endangered by a seemingly new Church that looks on them more as tolerable anachronisms than wise and useful elders. The priest, be-

cause of cultural changes, can no longer operate in relationship to his people from his former authoritative position or
status.

Everything Father says is no longer sacred, his faults are
not easily excused, and the demands made on him are
strongly personalistic. That is to say, his role as priest in the
Catholic community no longer protectively covers his faults
or inconsistencies. Neither does it obscure or cause him to
suppress unique strengths and talents. His ministry, now
examined with such active curiosity by so many different
people, no longer centers on a set of tasks or duties faith-
fully to be fulfilled. It centers rather on himself and how he,
as the Christian person who is a priest, can respond to any
and all of the needs of the people. The incarnational emphasis of this era demands that he reveal himself in his
work, that he give to his people not answers or directions,
but himself. This is obviously an awesome challenge since it
in effect says to the priest: you cannot relate solely through
ecclesiastical function, nor through a bygone tradition that
made you the authority on everything. You are, in many
ways, on your own as a human being among your fellow
human beings.

The younger clergy find this the kind of music which they
like to hear. In an age that has strongly endorsed the dignity
and meaning of the human person, they have little taste for
many of the authoritarian and impersonal aspects of the
now dissolving clerical culture. They are, however, still living in its structures because no others have been provided
on any large scale as yet. This has an inhibiting and depressing effect on many of them who find adjusting to the cleri-

cal life that has not yet caught up to the newer theology they learned in the seminary arduous indeed. They exhibit their discomfort in a variety of ways, some of them sullenly immature, some of them passionately committed to a new and better Church. Many, for example, reject out of hand everything that has the slightest relationship to an earlier era of priestly existence. They will not wear clerical clothes, they will not be on time or show respect for experience. They have little reverence for the pieties of the past. This annoys older clerics and the younger ones know it. It is a real acting-out of their rejection of the clerical culture I have described.

An interesting footnote to this is the apparent disinterest many young priests have shown for joining associations of priests in their dioceses. These associations have not seemed, apparently, to seek the values which they think are paramount at this time in history. The reasons for this may be complicated but one aspect of it is that most senates and associations have placed items regarding the security and status of the priest himself high on their agendas. This does not affect the younger priests in the way that it does his elder colleagues. He sees the future, rightly or wrongly, in a more open fashion and he sees the present as a time for a more personal and less tradition-bound exercise of the priesthood.

There is tension for the younger priests who have high personalist ideals because they find themselves somewhat frustrated by the still extant structures of a previous era. For example, rectory life is not satisfying to them when they want to live more closely with the people. The priests' house seems to them a barrier, a fortress of sorts that prevents them from breaking through into a new and more flexible style of life. They feel intensely the need to be closer to those they are called to serve. They are not satisfied with the old principle that their closest friendships should be with their fellow priests. They urgently want closeness with others and feel that they cannot live healthily without this. Because the vestiges of clerical culture seem to make this difficult and at times even unacceptable as an ideal, they mistranslate the consequent tension into a desire for marriage. This naive expectation that marriage will prove to be a solution for their problems is a sign that many of these young priests have not yet learned much about life and its vagaries. To them, however, it is a pressing difficulty. They want closeness with persons as part of their priesthood and they value this far more than the task-oriented, status-centered priesthood represented by clerical culture. The end of celibacy seems to them the only possible way to introduce the deep human relationships which they want in their lives. Putting aside other aspects of the celibacy question, it is clear that, unless newer and freer forms of priestly life are developed, the pressure of this issue will continue to mount. It is at least partially because the older clerical culture had such an attenuated and defensive attitude toward celibacy and closeness in all human relationships that the matter of celibacy is questioned deeply today. In an earlier stage in the American Church the emphasis in seminary formation and the code of priestly life was that the celibacy of the priest was to be preserved at all costs. The range and quality of relationships was narrowed because of this. Animal spirits were to be worked off in athletics and the clerical world was the only arena for "real" friendship. Women were a threat to integral virginity and were to be kept at an extraordinarily safe distance.

Incredibly typical of the retreat-master advice of that time was the injunction "always to keep the vesting table between you and a woman." I have always been fascinated by the gymnastic strategy implicit in this since most vesting tables are built against sacristy walls. In any case, a newer spirit sees this restrictive view of the possible range of celibate human relationships as unrealistic and unacceptable. The failure to explore the positive dimensions of celibacy as a state of healthy and open relationships with others has heightened rather than lessened the tension connected with it.

The statement of the Bishops of the United States on the question in November, 1967 is a classic failure in pastoral psychology. Framed in authoritarian tones, employing arguments far removed from the human condition, it succeeded in offending practically everyone, including many of the defenders of celibacy. What it failed to sense was that the celibacy discussion is a symptom of the massive cultural transition underway in the United States. Younger priests will shape a new style of service that will put them into more varied, independent, and closer relationships with their communities. The defensive posture of the older clerical culture is outmoded and, painful as it is for the older generation who lived in it with great dedication, is being put aside.

A new era in the nature of priest-people relationships is

developing and this will reinforce the need for the pastor to be a strong human individual who can give of himself in his ministry. The human resources of the priest will be the real focus for the effective priest of tomorrow. All the great conciliar ideals from freedom to collegiality can come to life only in the context of people in relationship to one another. The notion of Christian community and the function of the minister in developing and supporting it places his own self in the center of this Christian process. His cultic role can no longer be divorced from his personal presence among his people. Much of this will be discussed in later chapters. It is sufficient to grasp here the sociological and psychological dynamics which are forcing the priest out of a separate caste life into a communal, highly personal life of sharing deeply with his people.

This is no less true of the relationship between bishops and priests. Priests must constitute a college of men who participate in the priesthood of their bishop and this obviously dictates a restyling of their human relationships. If the bishop can no longer be the distant and all powerful prince, the priest can no longer be the passive-dependent and dissatisfied underling. None of this restyling can take place in an abstract theological realm. It takes place in the cruel midday sun of everyday life, in the development of healthier human relationships throughout the Church. There is an interesting built-in danger to senates and associations of priests at the present time. Many of them have come into being because of a dynamic of resentment as much as because of a dynamic of responsibility. That is to say, many of these organizations have, in some vague sense, pitted themselves against the bishop, as though the whole progress of the Church depended on their wresting concessions and permissions from somewhat reluctant and paternalistic ordinaries. This is to reinforce rather than reshape the father-son relationship of bishop and priest.

In other words, these associations which want to help move the church into the future, may, in fact, turn out to be the most conservative forces of all. This is not necessarily true but it surely is so wherever the basic pattern of relationship is one of preserving the false model of the ordinary as the father figure, the giver or withholder of good things to a basically expectant and therefore somewhat immature presbyterate. The associations and senates which have made healthy progress have achieved it because they have not attempted to change their bishop's personality, but have understood and tried to implement a responsible collegial relationship with him.

Pastoral psychology attains a new importance at this time when such basic transformations of the human dimensions of the Church are underway. An older clerical culture emphasizing a relationship of aloofness within authoritarian structures is yielding to a new age of more shared responsibility in a close and intensely personal manner. Pastoral psychology provides at least some of the insights that are needed for priests whose own personhood will be increasingly central to their ministry in the Church.

This is so because pastoral psychology begins with this emphasis on the priest as a man. It helps in understanding his incarnational role as the servant of God's People. It broadens our sensitivity so that we can better grasp not only what he does but also who he is. Psychology applied to pastoral work does not provide a new framework of techniques to protect the priest. Neither does it provide a psychological substitute for the Gospel message. It does offer the priest a means for understanding himself and his people as he tries to enter more fully into his role of mediator in a cultural setting that has transformed itself around him. Psychology can help the priest to sharpen the counseling and other relational skills that are so importantly a part of his ministry of the Word. There is no doubt that this discipline will help him to understand others, but the most important of its contributions will be that it helps the priest to understand and utilize more effectively his own personhood as an instrument and sign of salvation.

2

The Call to Imperfection

In one of his last short stories Frank O'Connor tells a tragic story of a young Irish priest's suicide.[1] The matter must be covered up, the determined pastor decides. Through coercion of the doctor and cooperation from the other curate and the undertaker, the deed is done and no one, not even the deceased's family, is the wiser. The surviving curate witnesses and participates in all this, his own reactions contained and unverbalized as the wistful ruse is accomplished. It is only after the funeral, as he turns back to his work again in the last line of the story, that he sighs "What lonely lives we live."

This story captures some of the possible loneliness of the pastoral figure whose isolation in a clerical-culture model of life is highlighted in moments of confrontation with the ultimate aspects of reality. This frustrating sense of being on the outside of human experience has been documented in many ways. It was, for example, one of the recurrent themes in James Kavanaugh's best-seller, *A Modern Priest Looks At His Outdated Church*. All his anger and anguish at being trapped in a cultural role he has grown to despise are caught in his cry *"Don't* call me 'Father.' Call me 'Jim,'

and make me know the reality that is life."[2] Indeed, one of
the reasons for the success of this book is that it expresses
the kind of anger many of Kavanaugh's fellow priests and
religious have felt but have been unable to phrase for themselves. They have experienced the crush of being caught in a
culturally delineated framework of expectation and response
which has prevented them from entering more deeply into
the lives of those to whom they would bring the words of
eternal life. For their part, the Catholic people have re-
sented the unfortunate distance between themselves and
their religious servants. Lay people are angry about their
traditionally passive and supposedly docile position in relationship to a clerical caste that seems far removed from the
reality of their life struggles.

All these occurrences are further examples of the high
personal price paid by both priest and people for the unfortunately stylized patterns that were described in the
previous chapter. All this takes place with pain that is the
greater because there is now a richer vision of the meaning
of the Church as a People of God who share life together.
The priest and religious have lived out parts in a scenario
that has lost meaning in the post-conciliar age. They have
suffered the consequences of being trained and assigned
positions in relationship to the faithful in a model for the
Church which possessed an inadequate understanding of
the meaning of the human person. It is little wonder that
priests could sigh "What lonely lives we live" since, according to this model, their own feelings were to be suppressed
by purposes of work or practice that obscured their genuine
personal needs. They have spoken these words resignedly,

a part of man. There were more noble and less noble aspects of man. Sexuality, for example, was a highly questionable dimension of life, an unfortunate necessity for the continuation of the species. Although we are slowly recovering from these misapprehensions, their effects are still widespread. A priest may theoretically understand that the Holy Spirit acts on man in his total presence in the human condition rather than just on some part of him, and still react quite differently, in real life, both to himself and to others.

So deep have been the effects of this conditioning process that many priests and religious still fail to sense their own unity in the human condition. Some, for example, view themselves after the light-house model of humanity. In this notion the important thing is the intellect, the beam of light that searches the environment for what it would identify and understand. Everything else, as in the lighthouse, is merely underpinning to support the intelligence. This is why there are so many merely intellectual approaches to man, approaches that are incomplete because they address themselves only to one part of what man really is. That is why so many priests have tried to live by their intelligence alone and have tended to treat shabbily and mistrustfully other aspects of their personality. The intellectual answers have never really been enough either for themselves or for others in the human condition.

Arising from this view of the human person was a model for personal holiness or religious perfection, nowhere to be found in the Gospels either, which offered an excessive concentration on self rather than on self in relationship to others. It also provided an almost exclusively external norm for determining spiritual growth. Perfection, in an anticipation of John Watson, the psychologist who fathered "behaviorism," lay in adopting external behavior that was without human blemish. This ideal made failings, or even the experience of quite normal human feelings, something quite horrendous. This static idea of perfection was and is quite uncongenial to human nature. Man and his fallible nature were to be conquered rather than fulfilled.

This is a dead kind of perfection, fine for statues which never shiver under a mantle of snow or blink in the spring sunshine, but not for man. A good example of this tendency, which led to so much emphasis on keeping external rules, is the matter of distractions at prayer. It would take all of one's time to record the incredible amount of energy people have put into the effort to remove distractions from their prayers. In fact, one of the staples of confessional matter for priests and religious was the recounting of their many failings in this regard. To translate something as basically human as distractability into a category of moral fault betrays a real misunderstanding of the way men are. Man, however, is eminently distractable and, most of the time, this is quite indeliberate and quite healthy. It is of man's nature to notice things out of the corner of his eye, to forge chains of association constantly. Otherwise, he probably would not have survived long after emerging from the cave. His distractability is one of his charms, one of his protections, and an indispensable aspect of his inventiveness and adaptability. If man were not easily distracted, if he did not ceaselessly scan his own inner and outer environment, he would be impaired in sensing danger around himself. He would seldom allow himself the luxury of a new thought or ever notice the link between apparently unrelated phenomena. He would hardly ever ask the questions that are the sparks of his creativity. Despite the obvious quality of these truths, generations of seminarians and religious have been instructed that part of their pursuit of perfection was the determined extinction of distractions. One might as well try to overcome breathing or seeing. The saddest part of this notion is that it has so needlessly centered people on themselves and on relatively unchangeable aspects of themselves. The result of this kind of strenuous effort can only be frustration and a mass of non-redemptive suffering.

Perhaps the worst consequence of this style of approach is the way it leads people to feel guilty and unforgiving about themselves as persons. This is the general effect of any code of perfection which relies on standards outside and genuinely foreign to human nature.

If we get man in proper focus we see him as a unit of intellect and emotions, soul and body, destined to work together or not to work very well at all. A human person, in a profound sense, is his body. He does not just inhabit it. His emotions are not detached and erratic human flappings, but the feedback of an individual person in relationship to all the events of his life. Man, in searching for self-knowledge, may more properly ask "What do I feel?" rather than "What do I think?" This is so because his feelings are indeed the reverberations of his whole person, the sensitive indicators of his individuality, and he need not be afraid of them. Indeed, without an open stance towards his emotional life, he will never be able to exercise adult self-control as an integrated person. He will instead be constantly controlled by feelings he does not understand, or he will use ultimately ineffective techniques of denial and suppression on them. Self-knowledge arises when we are sensitive to our differential reactions and realize that these are the signs of ourselves in relationship to life. "What makes me enthusiastic? What makes me angry? What would I willingly make sacrifices for? Why, when certain things are brought up in conversation, do I wish that somebody would change the subject?" Behind the answers to these kinds of questions lies our real personality.

The problem with the static model of perfection is, quite simply, that it expects man to be perfect. This is patently an impossibility for any creature whose best hope must always be for a relative kind of perfection. Man is not made to assume poses of unchanging perfection, but to grow from within as fully as he can in his necessarily imperfect human condition. Man is a mistake-making entity. He gets tired; he can feel afraid; he falls down and gets up again. He can fall short but he can also measure up. These truths are, in fact, the glory of the human person. Man can only love himself if he begins with a wholehearted acceptance of his limited self. This is not to accept failure but to accept humanity, even as Christ accepted and assumed it.

There is a great sense of relief for the priest or religious who can recognize that his call to give himself as a servant is basically a call to imperfection. It is perfectly healthy to be imperfect. This is the human condition, the only one available to us, and it is not to be despised but to be embraced as deeply and truthfully as possible. The rigid and unyielding demand for "perfect" behavior that has affected the attitude of so many priests toward themselves has tended to make them aliens to the human condition. They demand of themselves what human nature can never produce and end up expecting the same kind of behavior from others. This opens the gulf that has separated priests and people on so many occasions over the human issues that are at the very heart of genuine pastoral care.

But life belongs only to the truly human, to those with a feeling for what it means to share in the human struggle for growth. This idea of a relative perfection is not to approve of failures, although it invites an understanding of them. It is rather to reveal that the Spirit operates on man in the human condition and only in the human condition. When this fact is forgotten, man estranges himself from his own condition. In major league baseball, it is considered an outstanding accomplishment to hit over 300. In 1966, only two players from the ten American League teams managed to do this. That means, of course, that they failed seven times out of each ten times at the plate. And yet the 300 hitter is the premier athlete, the award winner. This is much more what perfection is like in the human condition.

It is a person's realization of his full potential, a fullness that will never disallow a large measure of imperfection. According to the rigid model that has had such marked influence in the formation of priests, one would expect to bat 1000 every season. The natural next step is to demand the same peerless performance in others. Failure to meet this standard leads to self-attack and to disappointment with others. A more reasonable expectation of the performance of human beings would necessarily structure a more realistic self-ideal as well as a more understanding view of others.

This basic notion of reasonable and humane expectations of human beings is extremely important in the exercise of pastoral care that is to be truly effective. The most important ingredient in this work is the person of the pastor himself. The only self that can be employed in the relationships that constitute pastoral work is the genuine self. This cannot be revealed if it is not understood and accepted by the priest himself. He can only turn against himself, as all too many priests do, when he fails because he has not really found his true personality in the human condition.

Before the pastor can reconcile others to God, he must reconcile himself sympathetically to his own person. The rich instrumentality of the pastor's humanity will never be employed if he is out of touch with or unforgiving toward his own humanity. His incarnation will fail if he evokes a stiff and unapproachable model of behavior that mistakes propriety for genuine love.

The real business of applying psychology to pastoral work concerns the deepening engagement of the priest's true self with the real and imperfect persons with whom he works. The Church as a People on pilgrimage is a caravan of sinners, not a parade of wooden soldiers. The action of God occurs where two or three persons gather in real relationship with one another. This is when the Spirit can touch them and lead them to a fuller life.

The priest who would apply psychology in his work for the People of God might begin by understanding himself and forgiving himself for his own humanity. He need not possess the offensively perfect smile or physique of those vitamin-filled clerics who sell breakfast food on television. He needs only to find and reveal himself as an understandably imperfect but also indispensable instrument of the Spirit in his service to the People of God who share the human condition with him, beings "darkly wise and rudely great."

Notes

1. Frank O'Connor, "An Act of Charity," *The New Yorker*, May 6, 1967, pp. 48–51.
2. James Kavanaugh, *A Modern Priest Looks At His Outdated Church* (New York: Trident Press, 1967), p. 26.

3

The Incarnational Role of
the Priest

The first understanding that Pastoral Psychology offers us is that the person of the priest or the minister is probably his most important asset in his work of ministering to God's People. In a real sense, it is what *he* does, not *what* he does that is important in carrying out the intensely human aspects of his work. No man ministers effectively from afar, his own person and feelings obscured or defended from public view. The man he is must be in it or there is no vital ministry at all. This incarnational challenge of the priesthood, emphasized so heavily in recent theology, has as its necessary prelude a real feeling for the human condition.

The priest has labored all too often in a role where he has felt unable to express his humanity very freely because of the immense expectations of his people on the correctness or holiness of his behavior. As Bowers has observed "the clergy suffer terribly from this need to be what they feel they should be, what they know their congregations expect them to be and what they know and feel themselves to be. They know their people expect them to be devout. They know they should be, and yet no matter how hard they try to find that innocence of faith and security we call devotion, it eludes them. As they continue to fail they become more and more angry."[1]

No other calling demands such a correspondence between the person's internal convictions and his external behavior. In no other profession is a disparity between the inner and outer world of the individual more severely condemned as hypocrisy than in those with pastoral responsibilities. As we have observed, the clergyman finds it difficult to forgive himself for his humanity. He thereby increases the tension within himself immeasurably. No real incarnational role, however, can be assumed except by a man who is familiar and understanding with his own personality.

This is not to lessen his ideal, which is more realistically drawn when he can accept and live according to his own personality more fully. The primary task for the pastoral worker is to be real in his relationships, to have something of himself that he can give away to others as he preaches to them. It is much better for him to have his imperfect and growing self available than for him to strain to present a facade of perfection that merely increases his own guilty feelings and proves ineffective in relationship to his people at the same time.

The very notion of imitating Christ represents a staggering ideal. How, indeed, is this accomplished? It is clear that there is no possibility of returning literally to the historical setting of Christ or to taking up the task of being a carpenter. Though he cannot transport himself back through the years and assume the garments and occupation of Christ, he is challenged to recreate something of the personality of Christ in his own world, to reflect through his own mentality the truths about man and his relationship to God that are the very essence of the Christian message. Another mistake, of course, is to assume external modes of behavior that are thought to be pious or representative of a mystical attitude toward man and his problems. This is the way the priest is often portrayed in the movies. In fact, it is the way Christ is often portrayed, as a rather distant and distracted personality with whom it would seem difficult to establish anything but the most shallow relationship. The trouble with making pious behavior our own is that it is not our own and there is no guarantee that it represents piety at all. Our experience might suggest that it represents an immature and defensive posture rather than any full bodied presence of a person given over to the action of the Holy Spirit.

Neither is Christ to be imitated by some paranoid identification with him, strangely present in many young priests who overemphasize the prophetic nature of their calling and presume to preach wrathful denunciations, delighting in confrontations at every turn. Not all the paranoid people in the world are in mental hospitals. The profession of the clergyman, along with politics and some others, has all too often attracted the paranoid individual whose identification with Christ is pathological rather than Pauline. It is rather the frenzied acting-out of a disturbed person who speaks the words of the Gospel not to free people for a fullness of life but to enslave them to a particular message or set of practices. These are often highly political in nature and the United States is full of roving Evangelists whose sermons reverberate with wars and rumors of wars.

It might be noted in passing that subtler forms of paranoid identification with Christ can also be observed in some clergymen. I have seen more than one who appropriates a single theme from Christ's life and tends to make this the whole of his own life. For example, I have seen priests in positions of authority who are able to sustain and even enhance their self-image by seeing themselves as misunderstood and misinterpreted by people who are too dense and hard of heart to pay any heed to them. They cover over the isolation that their ineffective human relationships have brought upon them and project their own difficulty in an exceedingly clever and self-serving way. They can see themselves following in the tradition of the suffering servant of Israel, the stone rejected by the builders, the prophet without honor in his own country. These notions remarkably buttress their own defensive system and allow them to continue in what are frequently basically maladjusted life styles. There is obviously something highly inappropriate in this selective identification with one scene of Christ's life, especially when it is used to close a man off rather than open him up to others.

If these devices fail, where can the priest or any Christian look for models that will enable them to reproduce the qualities of Christ through their own personalities? The real imitation of Christ is not something that calls upon a man to obscure or disfigure his own personality but rather to fulfill it. The priest or minister can imitate Christ in the quality of his relationships with others. This, after all, is one of the obvious meanings of the incarnation itself. Christ chose to live and grow among men and to reveal himself to them through his human personality in relationship to them. If the accidentals of this relationship cannot be recaptured with great authenticity in the present age, the qualities of sincerity and openness that are the primary human characteristics of Christ are not beyond our realization.

We represent Christ when we present ourselves to the world as fully and lovingly as possible. It is clear from reading the Gospels that Christ took on the human condition without compromise. This great lesson has been for some reason or other overshadowed in the process of history and it has only been rediscovered and reemphasized very recently by theologians. The genuine humanity of Christ and the deliverance of himself to all the demands of the human condition are part of the developing insights of contemporary Scripture scholars and theologians.

The lessons for the priest of today are clear and unambiguous. He must accept his humanity just as thoroughly as Christ did without despising the signs of his own necessarily growing and imperfect personality. The Gospels are filled with illustrations of how deeply Christ committed himself to the human condition. He did not exercise divine foreknowledge in his activity on this earth, he did not proceed like some magical figure who was immune to the processes of development that characterize human nature. He grew in relationship to his parents. "He was subject to them." He allowed himself to learn things. "He learned obedience through the things that he suffered." He experienced surprise and anger when this was appropriate, as when he drove the greedy merchants from the Temple of God. He did not suspend the rules of human nature but rather experienced their oppressiveness. He knew weariness at the end of a long journey—"He sat down by the well, worn out as he was from the journey," and a woman came along and he spoke to her.

The Gospel writer can hardly contain himself in telling us of Christ's attitude toward Martha and Mary and Lazarus. In the new translation available for the Gospel readings in the United States, the enthusiasm of the writer shows through clearly. He writes of Christ, "He loved them, he really loved them" (Jn. 11:5). This was not some glossy and static posture. This was the description of a living and breathing and deeply feeling human being. And he could grow lonely, as he did in the Garden of Gethsemane. Here he was moved to ask his followers why they could not stay up and keep him company for a while. In this same garden he revealed the unitary nature of human experience as he shuddered at the prospect of his forthcoming suffering and death. So thoroughly moved was he that his sweat became as drops of blood in a perfect revelation of the psychosomatic oneness of his human nature.

Endless citations could be given but the message would always be the same. If we are to reproduce the life of Christ in any way, the only agency available to us is through our own personality and the full participation of our personality in loving relationships with others.

This is a long and slow process of growth, this opening of ourselves so that we can give more of ourselves in the service of others. This is the way human beings develop and the priest's growth and development as a loving person can be no different. He reproduces Christ today by his own full embrace of his human nature, by forgiving himself for being subjected to its laws, and by his willingness to share himself deeply and fully with other people. The relationships in Christ's life clearly reveal for the priest a model that is really a challenge to his becoming more himself, rather than a pious automaton who tries to change, instead of fulfilling, his own human gifts.

The challenge for the pastoral figure is to take his own humanity into the midst of the human family and to become incarnate there in the only way that is genuinely healthy, as said before, through loving relationships with others. This cannot be accomplished unless his own personality, imperfect and growing though it may be, is engaged in this task. The priest is called to enter with a progressive lack of concern for himself into redemptive relationships with others. His ministry of the word is not limited to preaching from the safe remove of the pulpit. It also demands that he gives his person to others, that his words become flesh.

This is no easy task even for the man who is fully capable of understanding and accepting himself as he is and his human condition. It is a challenge that never ends, always demands further growth and further generosity on the part of the priest. It also, however, incorporates him into the human family in a healthy way so that he not only gives but receives love, he not only helps others to grow but grows in relationship to them.

The inevitable consequence, if he is to reproduce the re-

demptive cycle of Christ's life, is that this commitment to
incarnation is also a commitment to death. This is not a
depressing or dispiriting notion as much as a realistic understanding of the fact that anyone who is sincere about becoming incarnate must be ready to let many things die in
himself. This is the "old man" who, according to St. Paul,
must die in order that a new man may come to life in his
place. The death that the priest must undergo in his incarnate relationships to others centers on the defensive aspects of himself. These must crumble if he is to make
healthy and life-giving relationships with others.

What must die in him are the things that turn him in on
himself, the things that close him off from others, the whole
range of reactions which may lead him to save himself rather
than save others. The Gospel themes here are compelling
and these surely offer the guidelines for these redemptive
human relationships. It is the man who tries to save himself, after all, who ends up losing himself. It is the man who
is willing to lose himself, to undergo death, who really finds
himself. This is the dynamic core of redemptive suffering
and death that is so much a part of the incarnation of the
Christian minister in his work with other people.

This kind of suffering is very real and never becomes easy
to endure, this putting to death of the things that make us
selfish, but it is the kind of suffering that Christ came to
earth to teach men, the willingness to die out of love for
other men. This transcends the feeble concepts of mortifica-
tion which center on a rather self-contained practice of giving up sugar in one's coffee or similar behavior during a
season like Lent. The real death, the real mortifying of the

self, takes place in striving to love others more generously and more fully as each day passes. This is done within the context of the human condition and obviously will not be accomplished overnight. The pastoral servant must have patience with himself in this regard, realizing that his incarnation is an invitation to continued growth rather than an overnight development.

The redemptive cycle of Christ's life was completed by resurrection and this is no less true for the pastoral worker. If he embraces the human condition and exposes his own human imperfections in trying to establish loving relationships with other human beings, the priest will have to face and accept death to self, but this is inevitably followed by resurrection. New life comes to those whom he serves and fuller life for himself. All along the way the process of growth is reciprocal. It is deeply attached to the way he presents himself to other people. It is not all giving and, in fact, is the only real source of genuine growth and development for himself. This is the rhythm of the pastoral life: incarnation, death and resurrection, and there is no substitute for it. This is what makes his incarnation meaningful in the world of men. This is what breathes life into the liturgy he performs and into the relationships surrounding his sacramental ministrations. The incarnational role of the priestly figure is a calling to place himself, and only that which is truly himself, at the disposal of other people.

This is how the priest becomes an agent of the Spirit, an instrument of his intervention in human affairs. The Spirit makes use of the priest to the extent that the priest makes himself available through the opening of his own person to the promptings of the Spirit. This opening of the self that is the necessary prelude to the action of the Spirit in us is accomplished through the opening that takes place when we genuinely try to give ourselves in relationship to others. It is here that we are opened, not in some isolation from others, but only in the sincere surrender of ourselves to an incarnational role. This is how the Spirit reaches the world, through human relationships which require the dissolution of defenses and of the opaque quality that at once obstruct human incarnate reality and availability to the action of the Spirit.

It is in the priest's interaction with other men, through the instrumentality of his own imperfect self, that he fulfills one of the most important aspects of his servant role. Pastoral psychology sensitizes him to what is in progress on all the levels of his own personality. It helps him to understand the kinds of defenses which he can at times develop to confuse himself and to confound his people. The insights of psychology are nowhere more useful to the priest than in the patient development of a richer understanding of himself and the person he is in relationship to others. This is the human foundation for the work of the Spirit that is so importantly a part of his pastoral role.

Incarnation demands, then, a gradual fullness of the real person of the pastor in his relationship to others. This will necessitate his willingness to die to self in order that more of his real person can be present in truly loving them. This in turn will lead to resurrection in the form of new life shared by him and his people. Pastoral psychology high-

The Angelus
A Prayer For All

Leader: The Angel of the Lord declared unto Mary.

All: And she conceived of the Holy Spirit.

Leader: Hail Mary, full of grace, etc.

All: Holy Mary Mother of God, etc.

Leader: Behold the handmaid of the Lord.

All: Be it done to me according to Your word.

Leader: Hail Mary...

All: Holy Mary...

Leader: And the Word was made flesh.

All: And dwelt among us.

Leader: Hail Mary...

All: Holy Mary...

Leader: Pray for us, O holy Mother of God.

All: That we may be made worthy of the promises of Christ.

Leader: Let us pray:

All: Pour forth, we beseech You, O Lord, Your grace into our hearts, that we to whom the Incarnation of Christ, Your Son, was made known by the message of an Angel, may by His Passion and Cross be brought to the glory of His Resurrection, through the same Christ our Lord. Amen.

The Angelus is a traditional prayer honoring the role of Mary in the Incarnation of Our Lord. It is prayed in the morning, at noon and in the early evening.

Marian Year
1987-1988
Archdiocese of New York
His Eminence John Cardinal O'Connor, Archbishop

Our Lady of New York
Lady Chapel, St. Patrick's Cathedral, NY
Oronzio Maldarelli, Sculptor

lights the human elements in the redemptive cycle that represents the reality of pastoral incarnation.

Notes

1. Margaretta K. Bowers, *Conflicts of the Clergy* (Camden, N.J.: Thomas Nelson & Sons, 1963), p. 9.

4

The Dangers of Relevancy

The priest works in the world of persons. Here he finds himself at the fine point of tension between the sacred and the secular, at the joint of time that links now and the beyond. There is an unremitting existential strain connected with this that has been intensified by the extended discussion of the relationship of the priest to these domains. There is really no way to resolve the issue that arises in the debate about the transcendent and the immanent. To resolve the orientation of the priest exclusively toward the secular or exclusively toward the sacred would be to destroy the very creative position he occupies in society. It is for the priest to live on this shifting edge of culture, a man at home in what we may mistakenly consider to be two worlds. His challenge is to understand and put into focus the great issues about the all too solid flesh of a mankind that is called to surrender itself to the action of the Spirit. The priest is an interpreter and a guide as he shares in the great pilgrimage of the People of God.

This constantly exposes his own personality to hurt and to misunderstanding. It generates internal tensions which he may never successfully resolve. Research has indicated, however, that the creative person is indeed the one who can live with ambiguity, with polarized feelings that pull him now this way and now the other. The unfortunate overlay of clerical culture all but destroyed this rightful position of the priest in the very heart of society's struggles. It did this by offering the priestly caste a massive kind of security and a correlative temptation to stay within well-defined and unthreatening realms of activity. That is why there is a certain danger in relevancy, and many priests have experienced this already. The very world that seems to laugh at him and say that he is irrelevant because he pays no attention to the mighty issues of our time, can become quite upset with him when he does insert himself into problems like social justice and peace and war.

The world wants the priest to be relevant but not *too* relevant. Indeed, the fact that the priest meets a great deal of criticism when he betrays social awareness and speaks forthrightly about the world and its values suggests that he is identifying his role quite successfully. It is not a position of security and few priests are so self-assured as not to sense conflict within themselves when their own people, even perhaps their own families, tell them that the problems of the world are not their proper province. This is an understandable reaction from the older elements of the population whose Catholic world was well ordered and found a priest attending only to what could be vaguely termed "religious activity." But everywhere priests and ministers, as well as nuns and brothers, are committing themselves to the role of mediation and interpretation at the points in culture where the sacred and the secular do indeed clash.

This is just the point of these reflections. The new order of things denies the priest the security, and in some cases even a large measure of the respect, that was accorded him in a previous age. His relevance is achieved at a price that he must be willing to pay—living with ambiguity and uncertainty, moving constantly into the darkness with the light of the Gospel.

There are many priests who are very threatened by the newly developing image of the clergyman as a relevant person in society. Many do not comprehend, much less support, the colleague who is offering them the model of the priest of tomorrow. They want to maintain as much as they can of the well-ordered world of Catholicism. This is quite understandable and, in its own way, will inevitably lead them to confront their own consciences about the deep human problems of twentieth century America. These are unavoidable, and no man can really hide away from them. Any man who is involved with people as a leader and a molder of community finds that his chief work is in relationship with other persons. The virtue he must practice, then, must have a clear interpersonal expression or he is living in an abstract world of his own.

The priest of today is growing into a new role. The only priests who will survive into the future will be those who can effect the transformation successfully. This is a stage in the overall maturation of priests themselves. This growth will take place through his relationships with others and these will be found in this compelling and relevant arena of twentieth century living. More and more, whether he likes it or not, the priest will take a role in political, educational, and social questions. He will have to invest his work with the spirit of the Gospel and this will be reflected in the quality of his human relationships. This is indeed the sign of the presence of the priest in the world of men. He is a sign because he is guided by the Spirit and because he yields himself over as openly and honestly as he can to the Spirit's promptings.

More and more, the priest's role will not be identified solely by a set of religious tasks which he is to perform and which tend to keep him pretty much in the domain of what is called the sacred. The priest's role will be defined by the attitudes, the sense of values, and the personal convictions that he brings *as a man who is a priest* into any kind of work he does. No matter what the formal nature of his work is, if he is truly guided by the Spirit, he will be exercising his priesthood in it. This is why it makes sense to understand the possibility of priests' becoming deeply involved at all the points in culture where man is struggling with genuine questions of conscience. It explains the Anglican priest who labors side by side with atomic scientists in Oak Ridge, as they try to husband this new force for the world's good. It makes sense of the priest in any and every role when he invests his person in it and thereby exercises his priesthood at the same time. The work of priests becomes the work that priests do when they are genuinely illumined by the Holy Spirit in trying to bring a Christian interpretation of human problems to the issues they face.

There is a great danger of two things happening at the present stage of priestly development. First of all, those who have prized security and have become hardened in the aloof

life style of the formal clerical culture will be increasingly
threatened by new developments. They may prove to be
quite reactionary as they hold on to the roles they have
filled for years. There is no need, of course, for them to
condemn the development of newer forms of priestly life
and activity just because they feel they cannot change themselves at a late age. Indeed, it is fruitless for young priests
to attempt to try to change their elders who have been
denied the advantages of the kind of highly developed training available to the younger clergy. It is perfectly all right to
leave them alone and let them pursue their task of serving
the People of God as best they can. This will reduce the
need for the older generation to react defensively and un-
favorably toward newer developments.

There is also the danger of the possible development of a
new and more destructive kind of clericalism. There are
signs of this already. Instead of entering maturely into the
role of the priest who must mediate the growth of mankind's conscience on all the issues that confront our present
day culture, these priests seem more like angry young men
whose protests meet their own needs far more than those of
the world. This new clericalism has a dangerously boorish
character and could turn out to be far worse than the older
and more benign form. The Church really does not need
the disingenuous cleric who stands for nothing and has
nothing to give to others but an undisciplined self, a bastard
authenticity that is really not productive of growth and understanding in anybody.

These are the priests who seem to be fixated at a rebellious stage of growth, even as priests in the past may have

been fixated at a more passive level of development. In any case, they betray a complete lack of understanding of history and humankind. They are unwilling to expose themselves at the cutting edge where priests' lives must be led. They do not want to face the fact that all human problems are intensely complex and that the priest, of all people, must develop the sensitivity and patience needed for positive if gradual solutions.

The priest or other pastoral figure must understand and practice what we can describe as the interpersonal virtues. These relate him to the family of mankind. They put him on the spot, in a real sense, because it is only through the way he presents himself to others that he can ever bring anything of value to them. There is no Christian virtue that does not have an interpersonal aspect but, for purposes of illustration, it may be helpful here to consider the theological virtues of faith, hope and charity.

How one can consider these except in the world of persons is difficult to imagine. They can be described and analyzed intellectually but when we bring them into the world where we live they are all bound up with other human beings. There is nothing easier to preach about than this attractive triad. The difficulty, which underlines the immense difficulty of any human enterprise, lies in implementing these in our daily rounds. An investment of self is involved in bringing these virtues to life in our relationship with others. A man must lower his defenses, undergo a redemptive kind of death, in order to believe in, hope in, or love somebody else.

There is nothing easier to say than "I have faith in you,"

or "I trust you," and then to add silently to ourselves "but if you mess this up, I will never believe in you again," or "but I will keep an eye on you." It is also easy to say "I hope in you and this project you want to undertake," and to add "but I don't see how you can do it without me," or "but I don't think you will really make it." And it is almost effortless to say "I love you," and to add "if you love me in return," or "if you do the things I tell you." The difficulty is that all these bets are hedged, there is no real investment of the self made when faith, hope and love are professed in this way. Faith, hope and love do not, however, come in half-sizes.

These virtues do not nourish the human family when they are so diluted by our own hesitancies and fears. The only way these virtues really mean anything is if they are expressed through a person who is not afraid of the hurt that may come to him if he really involves himself in the things and people that need his trust, his hope, and his love. It is through his person in relationship to others that the Spirit works, but only if the man is willing to yield himself undefensively and, therefore, with great vulnerability to the needs of others. This is precisely why these interpersonal virtues are at the very heart of any relevant priesthood. They are the points of contact with human beings that enable us to have any kind of full or rich relationship with them. There is no meaning to a life that is lived on the surface, that depends on the manipulation of people, or on the cheap rewards of their approval. We are simply irrelevant when we confine ourselves to situations which are bland and without potential to hurt anybody.

The great sign of hope for the future is the fact that the priest is involved in all kinds of situations where any number of people may be hurt. This is indeed where the secular and the sacred converge, in the very heart of life as man struggles to make progress in humanizing himself. This is why the person of the priest is always in such great danger. Psychology gives us some insight into the fact that what stalls a man at living a more wholehearted life of faith, hope and love is that the investment that is required is one that must be made without charging any rate of interest and without even hoping for the return of the principal. These virtues are the human hallmarks of Christian witness. They make deep and steady demands on the person of the priest. That is why it is so important to see the priest clearly in his exposed position at the heart of human affairs. Indeed, the best measure of a priest's relevance is not whether he shouts prophetically or even looks somewhat pious. It is whether he willingly exposes himself to anguish and pain in trying to help others to grow in their own response to the Holy Spirit.

This is also why these virtues are sometimes in short supply. It is difficult to have faith in somebody when there is the danger that he may disappoint us. It is hard to have hope in somebody, to stand by him when he may turn away from us. It is exceedingly difficult to love somebody who, because we love him, has the power to hurt us. When we love anybody we give him that awesome power. It is to avoid this situation that we are tempted to move back into the old clericalism or into its new and strident version. Both types of clericalism excuse us from the interpersonal challenge that is inescapably a part of priestly presence in this world. The dangers of relevancy are the dangers of being crushed by our involvement with other human beings. By this I do not mean the irresponsible emotional involvement that all too often does become a part of a priest's life. I mean rather the patient giving up of ourselves even when we realize that we are consciously placing ourselves in danger while doing it. It is only in the interpersonal area that the central incarnational role of the priest can be lived with any effectiveness.

His enemy in all this is fear, the fear that can turn him back in search of security on one hand, or cause him to become a rebellious dropout on the other. Fear tends to paralyze us in the face of the challenge of loving others. It makes us turn away from the redemptive role that our priesthood urges on us because there is no place else to live it except in that very dangerous world inhabited by other human beings. But if good shepherds still lay down their lives for their flock, if a man still finds himself by being ready to lose himself, then the priest with a real pastoral sense knows that his mission is to this hazardous world of persons as a living sign filled with the faith, hope and love that flow from his real self.

5

The Priest and Community

The priest is described in the Documents of Vatican II as a leader and a builder of Christian community. It is this very role of leadership that some are trying to put aside, at least by implication, as they shed all the authoritarian trappings which they have found increasingly distasteful. The mistake, of course, is to identify authoritarianism with leadership. They are by no means the same thing and the priest cannot afford, in wishing to be dissolved somehow into a community which will generate its own priesthood, to put aside his obligations to be a healthy leader. His leadership is one that is not ordered to the authoritarian goals of controlling others but, as I have emphasized earlier, to the Christian goal of freeing them to find their full personhood in relationship with each other under the guidance of the Holy Spirit. The old model of the domineering priest is disintegrating along with clerical culture but some contemporary priests display an unjustifiable recklessness as they try to throw out everything that seems to belong to this former age.

Neither can the priest forget his call to form the community of believers around him. This means that he puts life into the community, which he can then genuinely celebrate in the liturgy they share together. The priest is the person who helps other people open themselves to each other and through this to establish and grow in trusting relationships with one another. The priest calls the Christian community into being in the sense that he alerts it to Christ's continued call. He does not do this if he is insensitive to the human factors that are involved in every contact with persons. He grasps the striking convergence of the insights of psychology with the theological principles of community that are being developed today.

This is not to say that there are no serious problems in the task of community building. These have always been problems and the process of a community's growth towards a healthy fullness has always been a slow and difficult one. At the present time there is a real hangup on the development of community which is caused, at least in part, by an imperfect understanding of Christian personalism. There are those who are so anxious to have community that they work at it in an unnatural and inhuman way. Many groups, including religious orders of both men and women, are striving to generate a kind of intimacy within their own communal situation which seems to go counter to the common sense of psychology and theology. There is, for example, an excessive investment in the human relationships within the community of religious. The relationships that remain solely within the community can never yield the kind of results that are expected of them in some of these efforts. There is a great employment of psychological techniques, from group dynamics to sensitivity training, in order to get people to open up to one another within their religious community or rectory. This is a kind of forced feeding that leads many healthy people to feel embarrassed at the inappropriate and unhealthy kinds of responses they are expected to make toward each other in the liturgy and other parts of their lives.

Human sharing does not come out of this kind of procedure, which is subtly authoritarian at its roots. The effort made to have people realize personalistic values is done in an aggressive and assaulting way and hardly leads to the goals which its overseers have in mind. There have been embarrassing public demonstrations of this, notably at liturgical conferences, where artificial practices of having people hold hands and go through other symbolic exchanges are supposed to develop some community feeling. People, however, have never become friends merely because they have held hands. In fact, it works just the other way around. Intimacy is something that is healthy but it arises out of relationship; it does not give birth to it. There is consequently a great deal of frustration because of the ultimately self-defeating nature of these practices. This is unfortunate because it tends to give "community" a bad name. At the same time it "turns off" the healthiest members who realize that part of Christian love is to know when to let people alone. These unrealistic efforts are well-intentioned but they are not tempered with a genuine sense of the way people live together. No community of persons lives in a superheated and super-charged emotional state.

The family, for example, lives in a rather casual way even in the healthiest of circumstances. The love that binds them together need not be manifested constantly or dramatically to reassure its members of its presence. Indeed, one would suspect that family therapy were in order if one observed some of these exaggerated phenomena in any household. This is community by contrivance and manipulation. It would be bad enough if all it did were to disappoint and frustrate the community members who are trying to participate in it. It is even worse, however, when it provides them with unhealthy and basically unworkable models which they may then carry over into their own apostolic work with the People of God. The truth of the matter turns out to be that they have shed real leadership but have assumed a new authoritarian position which pays little respect to the human or theological realities that underlie the development of any genuinely Christian community.

The priest is central to the development of the Christian community. The priest in his person is the focus and the mediator of the relationships of the members of any group, whether it is that of his parish, his study club, or his classroom. It is because the priest can possess his own person and can give the gift of that to other people that he can awaken in them a sense of their own personhood which they can then share more readily with others.

Our most attractive suburbs are often filled with people who live very defensively with one another. They tend to live in competition, their relationships pivoting on the fear that one's neighbor might excell oneself in attaining some sign of status. This generates a kind of fear that permeates the entire community and often makes it very difficult for neighbors to share anything on a very deep level. In a highly mobile society, where neighbors are coming and going all the time, this situation is only made all the more crucial.

People need each other, however, and manifest this in many ways. Their chief difficulty is in handling the defensive reactions which come to them almost unbidden when they are forced to face each other in open relationship.

This is why the priest's presence is so significant. His word and his person can call these people together. He becomes a dynamic force that enables them to reach each other through the mediation of his own person. When the priest can present himself to his people as an open and receptive person, as a man who can reach into the lives of others with sensitive understanding, then he is available for a deep relationship with them as individuals. The people can sense in the priest the kind of pastoral presence which enables them to lower their defenses and discover the rich possibilities of their own personal lives at the same time.

The priest offers to his parishioners the opportunity to form relationships outside themselves which are free and open and undemanding. These are relationships of love, not of frenzied emotional demand for some kind of rootless brotherhood. The priest who is mature is available for many deep relationships of this nature. He becomes an agent of the Spirit because it is through his relationship with the individual members of his parish that they are opened to the influence of the Spirit themselves. When they cannot reach each other because of fears and the competitive stress of culture except in a somewhat destructive kind of way, they can reach the priest who is fully alive and sensitive to them in the human situation. His personhood becomes a mediating force which enables them to find each other in healthy relationships because they have learned something about the Christian style of relationship through their experience with the priest.

He does not do this by artificial technique, by creating organizations that demand face to face relationships for which people are not prepared. In many ways he disposes them and helps them to acquire the kind of strength they need to reach through him to find each other in a close and healthy way in the Spirit. This is no small accomplishment. The priest is called, in the formation of community, to be a catalytic force, an instrument of grace in developing the human bonds of community. The priest enables his people to overcome their defenses and to begin to trust one another as they begin to see each other in a clearer and more realistic light. In a sense, then, the priest must be able to pull himself back from these relationships, and allow himself to diminish, as his community grows stronger in their sharing with each other. He does not dominate but he does lead and create the conditions that free people for a response to the Spirit, the very soul of any Christian formation.

It is in the discharge of this role of forming community that we may come to see celibacy as extremely important. Unfortunately, the Church will probably go through the process of altering the requirement of celibacy only to find that this change will not solve the problems of the priesthood it has been guaranteed to solve. But this is the way history is made and, if the true values of celibacy are then rediscovered, it will have been a useful if painful experience. Celibacy, however, presents the priest as an available human instrument of the Spirit in the development of community, an open person, unobstructed in relating to others by over-investment in himself. This is the position that many psychotherapists try to create for themselves in dealing with their patients. They attempt to control the effects of the primary relationships in their own lives so that they can present the fullness of their own person in the therapeutic relationship to the patient. There is a celibate quality, then, to the work of the psychotherapist as he helps the other find himself in relationship to his own person. This is precisely one of the dimensions of the priestly role that is notably augmented by sincere and positive celibate dedication.

This kind of celibacy, of course, cannot be a defensive posture aimed at preserving the priest, like the contents of a time capsule, unscarred by the experiences of life. It also underscores the need to transform structures within the Church so that the priest can, in fact, enter into the lives of persons in a more direct and a freer way. The priest who is fully grown presents, then, not merely an heroic or eschatological sign to his people in his celibacy, but the kind of human presence at a deep level in their lives that makes him truly a source of the Spirit for them. Through his genuine, non-possessive relationships the priest frees his people to exercise their own priesthood with each other. This is freedom through the Spirit, the freedom to respond to each other with something more than the superficial manners and styles of relationship that are so dead and unsatisfying. If Christianity represents the reality of a continuing revelation through its human community, this revelation cannot occur unless the Christian community attains a genuine measure of open relationship. Without this kind of sharing and without the kind of revelation that comes only on the condition that the community is composed of freely responding persons, there is no presence of the Church at all.

The importance of the person of the priest is underscored by these reflections. His understanding of himself, of the development of his own human consciousness, his ability to share his manhood in an open and available fashion makes him a bridge between people which they can cross to find each other and thereby establish the Christian community. The priest's task is to develop a growing awareness of his own human potential and of his own receptivity to other persons. This can only be achieved if he is willing to yield up the defenses that block his fullness of incarnation in relationship to them. The pastoral person is not meant to live a lonely life but one that is constantly involved at a deep and meaningful level with the persons who surround him. His celibacy, properly understood as a positive and open presentation of himself in order to further human relationships, can be an asset rather than a liability for him. Psychology can provide the priest with many of the insights he needs to understand his unique function in the human community, a function that can be supplied by nothing less than his whole personal involvement as the leader and shaper of the Christian community.

6

The Priest as a Professional

The American priest is somewhat reluctant about being classified as a professional person. This is so for many reasons, among them the feeling that the priest and his work are at a level that is somewhat different from that of lawyers, doctors, dentists or social workers. The priest tends to place these occupations in the secular domain and to perceive himself as representing the added dimension of the sacred. In fact, as was discussed in an earlier chapter, the priest lives at the very point where these areas of concern overlap. Priests are sometimes shy of the term professional for another reason. It seems to them to imply a somewhat cold and stylized approach to human persons, the kind they see reflected in crowded doctors' offices where heavy schedules seem to diminish the personal nature of medicine, or in the reserved or calm approach of the legal mind which strives always to remain emotionally uninvolved. The priest has an instinctive feeling that he cannot get caught in this professional trap because his relationship to his people cannot be merely one of giving them a specific marketable service. His is a concern for the whole meaning of their lives.

The reluctance of the priest to accept these connotations

of professionalism is understandable but they reflect only a partial comprehension of what that term implies. The priest is being moved by culture toward a more professional position in society whether he likes it or not. This means that the standards of his education and the integrity of his personal response as a priest must be on a level with those expected from his colleagues in the other professions. To admit the validity of this requirement of a professional image and attitude in no way diminishes the value the priest may perceive in preaching a transcendent message or in trying to deepen his total personal commitment to his people.

Indeed, professionalization in priestly training and in the conditions of priestly life is the only sure way to guarantee that these latter goals will be even minimally achieved. The priest loses nothing in wanting to be professional in his style of relationship because this indicates his determination to achieve both wholeness and excellence of performance in his life. In another age these bore the rubric "holiness" and "carrying out the duties of one's state in life." What is important, of course, is the overall attitude of the priest toward himself. Does he take himself seriously, both in preparing himself and in carrying out his pastoral function, or does he do this in some approximate and poorly disciplined way?

There is a considerable body of evidence to indicate that too many priests have not had a sufficiently professional attitude toward their work. They have been protected by the whole atmosphere of clerical culture which tended to insure a respectful response by their people even when they performed their duties in less than polished fashion. If a priest stumbled through his sermon, or seemed an "absence" rather than a "presence" to his people, they were ready to excuse him. "Father is sick again" or "Father is so busy" or "Father leads such a lonely life" constitute a familiar litany from the golden age of clerical culture.

This was not all the priest's fault, of course, and a good deal of his own uncertainty about professionalism stems from his highly unprofessional training and apprenticeship in the priesthood. The training was largely intellectual and done at a studied remove from flesh and blood people. His apprenticeship in his first years in the priesthood was profitable or not, depending on whether he lived with priests who took an interest in helping him to develop himself in a responsible way. All too often, however, he was merely expected to catch on to the routine as best he could, to keep his own counsel, and to wait for the day when age and seniority pushed him into a more respectable status in his life career.

As an example of the weakness of his training, the experience of medicine is quite interesting. In a careful study of the development of the professional self-image of the doctor, Huntington suggested that the most important element in its development is the progressive placement of the student physician in a position of responsibility for sick patients.[1] There has hardly been any analogue for this in the training of priests. Few of the apostolic programs now currently in vogue in houses of training have anything but the most cursory supervision of the essentially priestly activities of the seminarians who participate in them. This whole side of responsible professional behavior in dealing with human beings has been handled from an acutely intellectual view-

point. It is no wonder that the development of professionalism has been awkward and inconsistent for the Catholic
clergymen in the United States.

The characteristics of an individual who has a truly professional attitude toward his work spring from the way he
presents himself in relationship to those whom he serves.
His is a responsibility for the integrity of the service he performs. This means that he is presenting the best of himself
to others, that he has done his homework, and is not talking
or preaching off the top of his head. Professionalism demands that he continually develop himself through ac-
quaintanceship with the journals and documents of the
Church. This is the normal channel for the continued
education of the other professions and, while it can be a
staggering job to keep up with new techniques and developments, it is of the very essence of professionalism to accept
seriously the responsibility to do so, either through reading
or through participation in advanced courses and work-
shops. Part of the professional obligation of the diocese or
religious order is to develop, at whatever costs, adequate
programs of continuing education to aid in the development of the priest as a professional person. Not nearly
enough has been done to provide continuing education
programs for priests and religious in the United States.

The professional person, then, must have an underlying
serious attitude toward himself as he faces his responsibility
toward those whom he serves. He cannot present an ill-
prepared self and think that he is giving much to his people.
He cannot merely extemporize, then label it "fruitful experimentation," in the liturgy or in any other aspect of

Christian life. The professional sees that experimentation is not done without planning or without providing the means for evaluating the process and the outcomes of the experimentation. Experimentation in the United States, however, has hardly had a professional face. It refers mostly to things that people carry on in private, apparently to their own delight if not to the welfare of the People of God.

It is equally unprofessional for the diocese or the administrative officers of religious orders to look on experimentation as undesirable and to fail to provide the professional setting in which it can be carried on intelligently. This contributes as much as anything to the failure of professional development. Research cannot be done by the careless design of questionnaires or the naive polling techniques that have been used so extensively in the United States on important questions connected with the priesthood. Postcard polls on clerical celibacy do not constitute careful research. This failure has been as much on the side of those anxious to preserve celibacy as on the side of those who wish to modify this requirement. In any case, informally gathered data are hardly respectable, except to aggravate feelings connected with the discussion. This is to employ a research model aggressively and destructively. This is the very antithesis of professional behavior. There is a discipline required in research and a willingness to take time and invest funds so that it is carried out properly.

A professional meets certain standards in the way he implements his relationship with those who come under his care. These are closely related, of course, to the way he prepares himself for his meeting with them. It is not uncommon to find a surgeon studying very carefully before a major operation. This is a sign of his sense of responsibility toward himself and his skills. Homework is always difficult and ordination does not excuse a priest from it. In specific situations he must take the time to acquire the kind of information or knowledge he needs to participate meaningfully in a discussion. He cannot generalize out of his own feelings on any subject, whether it be on peace, social justice, or the financing of Catholic education.

Argument by emotion or in increasingly louder tones is unprofessional. Within the Church, of course, the laity can be as guilty of this as the priest. It is, however, a clear aspect of the priest's professionalism to prepare himself for the specialized moments in which he responds to the needs of his community. This can be in his preaching or in his counseling; it can be in his administration of the sacraments or in his writing the parish bulletin. It takes reflection and perhaps wide reading to communicate intelligently on the issues that concern people in their lives today. To this end, the priest must have the professional openness to see that he does not corner the market on all knowledge and that his professionalism is best revealed in a readiness to learn in the very situations in which he is serving.

There are a number of incidental characteristics of professional behavior which the priest who takes his role in the people of God seriously also exhibits in his own life. The real professional, whether he is an actor, a lawyer or a surgeon, is on time for his appointments, answers his mail with reasonable promptness, returns phone calls, and makes decisions about invitations, whether to make a speech or go to a party, with sensitivity to the needs of others. There is a discipline of life reflected in this behavior that is absolutely necessary in the life of the priest. This is particularly relevant for the new generation of clergy who are anxious to shed some of the worst aspects of the formalities of the past. As I have mentioned before, their passion to do this sometimes leads them to give up good manners. They are not, for example, truly professional or truly adult when they present themselves on public occasions in the styles of private recreation. This may seem to them an engaging symbol of casualness but it often strikes the world as merely gauche. They cannot really cast off their obligations to be professional by claiming that they just want to be one of the people. This is a fundamental failure to grasp responsibilities of the professional and dignified manner, which is not the same as stuffiness or hauteur, that should characterize the gift of themselves through service to others.

Probably the most important professional characteristic that should be reflected in a priest's life is his sense of responsibility for the welfare of others. This is at the heart of the kind of relationship he must have with others if he is truly to be an instrument of the Spirit in their regard. For whatever reason, this sense of responsibility for the person of the other is notably lacking in too many areas of priestly life today. Responsibility for the person of another is the characteristic of a professional but, more importantly, it is the mark of somebody who knows how to love. If there should be one distinguishing characteristic of the priesthood, one sign of the transcendent world which he hopes to represent, it should be in his awareness of the value and meaning of love. His relationship of service is fundamentally a loving one in which he gives not only his particular skills but, through them, his whole person to those whom he serves. His whole person must be available so that others can establish relationships that are genuine and satisfying for them in their particular moment of need.

Professionalism may seem to be a dirty word or to have uncomfortable connotations to the priest who thinks that love is communicated in a protoplasmic and shapeless presentation of the self to others. This is the behavior of someone who is immature, who does not sense the presence of others in the world around him because he is totally consumed with his own needs and his own outlook. This is thoroughly unprofessional and decidedly unchristian. Numerous examples of this kind of outlook could be offered.

Perhaps, in current clerical life, it is best evidenced in the pseudo-personalist activity of those who make "love" a big thing in their lives and insist so much on their need for fulfillment in this regard. They have a hit-and-run technique with people which enables them to use others, especially women, for a time and then to back away from the relationship when it seems to demand something in the nature of continuing responsibility from them. But love is continuing responsibility, not just high moments of honeymoon-like experience; it is the patient and constant effort to share the struggles of others, not merely in so far as they fascinate or reward us, but with a dedication to the other which does not permit the priest to pull out of the relationship when it becomes difficult or trying for him.

This mark of professionalism, the sense of giving oneself honestly and seriously in service to others, should be one of the signs of the Christian witness the priest gives in a world which has enough faltering loyalties. He should be a model of professionalism in an environment where shoddy workmanship and superficial performances too often pass for art and accomplishment. The business of the priest is human relationships. Much of his time is spent in counseling or in other similar interactions. The more the priest can sensitize himself to his own role in these relationships, the more he can understand the depths of his own potential as a human being, the more thoroughly will he give himself over to the work of the Spirit and become a source of the Spirit for his people.

A professional attitude is necessary for any person who mediates the anguish of the community of mankind. This demands highly disciplined skills, a readiness to learn, and an openness to the self which recognizes one's own personhood as the most important element in developing life-giving relationships with others. This professional attitude does not arise solely from the intellectual study of textbooks, nor from mastering the categories of psychiatric diagnosis.

Many priests approach the study of pastoral psychology with the notion that this will help them to learn a great deal about other people. That is undeniably true but it is only part of the purpose of pastoral psychology. The priest who takes seriously the implications of the study of psychology, will soon find that the person he learns most about is himself. He must confront himself as a man and be willing to look in the dark corners of his own motivation and at the subtle fears that can so markedly affect the way he is able to present himself in relationship to other people.

If he is to give up his amateur standing, he must be willing to take a good hard look at himself. This is in the great tradition of ascetical literature which has always placed thoroughgoing self-knowledge as a primary requirement for anybody interested in the life of the Spirit. The insights which illumine our understanding of theology do not provide merely techniques. They suggest that the pastor begin with a steady self-examination that leads to further understanding and possession of himself. It is much the way a batter who is in a slump may study movies of his stance at the plate, or the way a golfer with a bad hook may have to study his position in addressing the ball. What he is doing wrong may be hidden from his own consciousness until he takes a searching look at himself. So too it is with the priest who wants to take on responsibility for the welfare of others. This is not a shallow status-oriented kind of professionalism, but the highly demanding and mature attitude of the man who understands something of the solemn nature of his calling to be a loving presence in the People of God. It is to help him understand his own person in his human relationships of pastoral ministry and to aid him in being more professionally effective with others that the following chapters are presented.

Notes

1. Mary Jean Huntington, "Development of Professional Self-image," *The Student Physician*, ed. Merton, Reader, Kendall Cambridge, Mass.: Harvard University Press, 1957), pp. 179–187.

7

The Priest Looks at Himself

---

*The man who protects himself from the
raindrops will never find out how
beautiful they are—*
JAPANESE PROVERB

The priest and religious, even after years of examining their consciences, still have difficulty in knowing and understanding themselves. It is hard for them to see themselves in action in life with other people. Part of the reason for this springs from the fact that their years of examination have been almost exclusively intellectual in nature and thus have focused on only one aspect of themselves. Add to this the traditional emphasis on individual actions rather than on any comprehensive *pattern* of individual behavior, and the difficulty of getting a full view of oneself is even more obvious.

There has always been an emphasis on acts committed or omitted, on whether they were weighty or trivial, right or wrong, pleasing or unpleasing to God. This kind of examination of the self has been carried out with the idea of a standard or yardstick outside the individual against which he could measure himself. The emphasis is thus on behavior and its modification from the outside rather than on the roots of behavior and an understanding of the internal dynamics which give rise to it.

This emphasis, over-intellectual and over-statistical in nature, does not help the person to understand his behavior with any sense of continuity between his past self, his present reactions, and his future possibilities. It makes it difficult for him to sense the overall orientation of his own person in relationship to others. This is really the heart of understanding oneself, the understanding of the total human personality in its whole range of relationship with other persons. This latter pattern or style of reactivity genuinely presents the profile of the individual in action in life. This is very closely related to recent concepts about sin as essentially an orientation of the whole self toward or away from God. This is not summed up as much in individual actions as it is in the whole direction of one's life.

Real knowledge of the total self only comes when the individual can find out something about how he places himself in relationship to others. He must see what he is really doing to them, or giving to them, or even hiding from them. He must link the actions he performs to the feelings that motivate them in order to get a sense of his own presence in the human family. This is where the priest, whose person is so central to his pastoral role, must begin. The prospect of taking a long, hard look at himself and at the affective roots of his behavior may not be attractive. Self-examination seldom is. This is, however, an aspect of the death that the priest must undergo if he is to rid himself of the defenses that prevent him from accomplishing the most essential work of his ministry, that of establishing loving relationships with other human beings.

There are many styles of relationship, of course, and wise men have struggled through the centuries to give us descriptions that would aid us in understanding human behavior more accurately. Psychology and psychiatry have specialized in trying to uncover and make intelligible the various strands of motivation, from primal urges to creative insights, which make man what he is. Anybody must begin an examination of himself with a readiness to find some things which are unpleasant and other values which are as good as they may be unexpected. There is a quality of openness, of willingness to face ourselves in the stance we normally assume in relationship to others, that is indispensable for the priest whose whole work is in relationship to others. A priest must be ready to find whether he is trying to control others or protect them from the consequences of their own freedom, and thus deny them a fundamental human right. He must discover whether he really respects their separateness from him and their wholeness as unique human beings who are struggling to become more independent and responsible for themselves.

The disintegration of clerical culture has made the authoritarian stance one that can no longer be comfortably assumed in relationship to the People of God. It does not command respect in an age where people are willing to embrace the free responsibility for their own lives. The authoritarian personality has been the subject of much psychological analysis. A relatively recent study by Weatherby reveals the characteristics of this authoritarian personality as typically adolescent and immature.[1] He has little inclination to act autonomously, to think deeply about himself and to admit his own inner feelings. He is (ironically) dominated by a desire for dominance over others, and an excessive wish to maintain order and system in his own affairs. This gives a classical picture of the position assumed by many clergymen in ages when very few human institutions believed in democracy or the power of individual people to govern their own lives. There are still vestiges of this demanding authoritarianism in the Church.

Weatherby's study, along with much other research, suggests that this posture is basically a highly defensive one for the person who employs it. It is a facsimile of strength through power that masks a substratum of uncertainty and inadequacy. This is the refuge, then, of the undeveloped and ungrown person, and can hardly be a fitting attitude for the priest who is called to serve rather than manipulate the people of God. Authoritarianism hardly needs any more denunciation. It is useful, however, to see that it is a terrible distortion of the meaning of genuine authority, which in itself implies a far healthier kind of relationship toward others on the part of the one who exercises it. Genuine authority refers to relationships which help other people to grow. It implies a continuing presence that is freeing rather than controlling in nature. Genuine authority cannot be exercised by the individual who is not healthy and capable of making mature relationships with others. He will almost always distort it into a form of authoritarianism in order to support himself. This is to put others to death rather than to help them grow.

The authoritarian position is closely linked to many styles of relationship that have been handed down through the generations of clerical culture. The priest was the sure source of knowledge, the one who knew best about what we should read and look at, and think about. The danger in this position is that it tends to reinforce passivity on the part of others. This is the counterpoint to the subtle rewards it gives to the one who finds that it is his only possible way of relating to others. The authoritarian attitude also tends to ignore persons and to focus on their problems from an outside point of view. This is hardly even therapeutic.

It becomes easy to see why there is in this present age such a reaction to the authoritarian style of relationship. It frustrated growth and went counter to any attitude of genuine faith, hope or love of others. It aimed at control through manipulation which was basically gratifying to the authoritarian person himself. Unfortunately, too many immature men and women have inherited positions of authority to which they could only bring their own inadequate life style. This tended to destroy the vitality of authority as a healthy aspect of life and consequently to cause great harm to all the relationships within the People of God.

When an immature person gets into authority he necessarily acts out his own defensive life style and this has very little to do with anybody but himself. This is why so many superiors are under such great threat when their subjects propose a model of collegial decision-making to them. For immature superiors authority has been a reward that has reassured them of their worth and has tended to reinforce their whole faulty way of relating themselves to the world. This is a prime example, then, of an attitudinal position with which everybody in the Church is all too familiar. It is a stance that is no longer tenable. Indeed, it is unfortunate that it was unquestioned for so long. It is a classic illustration of how the priest must *not* relate to his people if he is going to help them to grow to a greater fullness of themselves and to a greater sensitivity to the action of the Spirit.

If the priest is really anxious to find out about himself and the ways in which he relates to others, he may begin by trying to sense whether there are any vestiges of this authoritarianism still present within him. Many of the so called liberals of today are quite as authoritarian as the unhappy and ineffective monarchs of yesteryear. They may have changed the circumstances and settings in which they exercise it but its dynamics are exactly the same. They need to have people accept and follow them, they desperately need disciples who can be made over in their own image and likeness. It makes no difference that now the cause may have very egalitarian overtones if the inadequate authoritarian dynamic still operates from within.

All the talk about freedom and collegiality that fills the air has not been implemented fully as yet. Authoritarianism dies hard and, like the intractable virus which develops immunity to wonder drugs, authoritarianism develops new strains as fatal as the older and more easily recognized disease. There are those, for example, who fight for dialogue when they really mean monologue. They fight for freedom as long as people accept the values or practices which they now urge upon them. They will fight the old authoritarianism as long as they really don't have to trust, or believe in, or expose themselves to the terrors of really loving other people.

Beyond an examination of just how much authoritarianism may be left in any one of us, there is a need to take a broader look at the habitual way in which we relate to other individuals through our apostolic work. We can look at them from the outside, from what the psychologists term "the external frame of reference." We can, on the other hand, try to get a glimpse of what it is like for them on the inside, or from "the internal frame of reference." Much as we may espouse our belief in entering sensitively into the world of the other, we are so accustomed to looking at others from the outside that it is a difficult position to attain. In general, one is tempted to look at life from one's own viewpoint and to evaluate it according to one's own experience or one's own values. To be open and honest and to put aside our own self-invested view for a moment may seem a simple thing but it is extraordinarily difficult.

It is so much a part of us to judge others that it is difficult to stand back and take a look at ourselves even as we are engaged in the evaluative process. It seems so altogether right after a lifetime of acting in this way. We are like the American tourists walking through the forum in Rome who say, in a betrayal of their evaluative American attitudes, "Wouldn't you think they would clean this place up?" There are numberless pieces of advice which we begin with the words "The way I see it," or "The way we did it when I was in school," or "The way we did it when I was a kid," or something quite similar.

This is made the more difficult for the priest because, as a part of his education, he has been trained intellectually to make judgments about moral rightness or wrongness. He has been trained to stand in the external frame of reference and to look at behavior from an objective and outside viewpoint. This has its place when one is called upon to render judgments about moral situations but it may not be quite so helpful in the realm of establishing healthy human relationships. The priest need not always be the judge.

He is not, in fact, the expert on all human affairs he may presume himself to be because of his seminary training. That would be an awesome assumption, to place oneself in the position of being able to judge quite accurately what is appropriate or inappropriate for others to do, to say, or to be concerned about. Yet, these attitudes can be very deeply a part of us without our genuinely sensing them. If someone should question them, we would probably get defensive and try to justify the attitude we have. This is not to deny our rationality or our ability to judge in an imperfect and human manner. It is to state, however, that the viewpoint of the outsider, the man who cannot enter into the present situation or into the lives of those with whom he works, will probably keep him permanently on the outside of other people. It will not be the attitude of openness needed for the person called to be the leader who knows how to exercise authority so that it helps others to grow to their own fullness. It is not the attitude or orientation of the individual who is called to form the Christian community.

One of the most helpful and simple devices for a priest is to examine himself according to the schema presented by Porter. Here is a non-exhaustive but stimulating framework for examining one's habitual attitude and position toward others. Porter offers a counseling pre-test which reveals a man's relative score on these variables. It is the variables themselves, however, which are of particular interest to us at this point. Four of the attitudes presented by Porter are these:

E—Evaluative. A response which indicates the counselor has made a judgment of relative goodness, appropriateness, effectiveness, rightness. He has in some way implied what the client might or ought to do: grossly or subtly.

I—Interpretive. A response which indicates the counselor's intent is to teach, to impart meaning to the client, to show him. He has in some way implied what the client might or ought to think: grossly or subtly.

S—Supportive. A response which indicates the counselor's intent is to reassure, to reduce the client's intensity of feeling, to pacify. He has in some way implied that the client need not feel as he does.

P—Probing. A response which indicates the counselor's intent is to seek further information, provoke further discussion along a certain line, to query. He has in some way implied that the client ought or might profitably develop or discuss a point further.[2]

The external frame of reference underlies all these positions even though at first inspection this may not seem to be so. It may be helpful to discuss briefly the ways that these attitudes may be manifested in the life of a priest.

The evaluative stance clearly indicates the choice made by the priest to deal with the situation or the persons in terms of a moral judgment. In passing this kind of a judgment, whether it is about what the individual should talk about or whether a decision made by the individual is right or wrong, the priest is standing outside of him rather than along side of him as the person tries to get a better look at himself. This frequently happens when the priest is dealing with personal problems, the symptoms of which are described by the troubled individual who seeks the help of the priest as a counselor. If the priest focuses too much on the symptoms, he may fail to see them in relationship to the individual who is experiencing them. He then fails to sense their significance as the outer indications of inner dynamic behavior.

The passing of external judgments hardly moves the process of counseling forward but it does serve one purpose which may not be immediately obvious to the priest in this situation. It reinforces him in a position of distance and authority. It may quite subtly and unconsciously prevent him from giving the fullness of his attention in this situation because he has already erected a framework of relationship that goes counter to this. The evaluative viewpoint tends to support the priest as a knowledgeable person, whose advice is sought on a difficult matter. The rewards, in other words, may be more for the priest as the counselor rather than for the individual who is talking with him.

The interpretive attitude is that assumed by the amateur psychologist or psychiatrist who has dabbled enough to be quite dangerous in dealing with other people. This is not the response of the person who has had to face life in all its seasons as much as the response of a person who sees life in an over-simplified and naive fashion. Once again, the priest places himself in an evaluative and highly authoritarian position. He looks from the outside and runs the danger that he may put things together at a pace that is too rapid for the person or persons with whom he is dealing.

Most of us resent and resist others when they interpret our behavior, even when they are correct. To interpret the behavior of another is a skill that is exercised with great prudence and judgment even by the most expert therapist. The priest who has a smattering of Berne's *Games People Play* often indulges in an interpretive analysis of the behavior of others. Quite frequently he invests too much in the belief that this kind of intellectual interpretation will be enough to help the other solve his or her difficulty. He is befuddled and frustrated when he finds that his interpretation is rejected. The worst result of this kind of habitual stance, the stance of the all-knowing expert, is that it may seriously damage the possibilities of a more open and healthy kind of relationship with the other. It is not easy to put aside an attitude which can be so indirectly rewarding to the priest because it presents him as a quite superior and skillful person. The possibility that this attitude may be dangerously obstructive is seldom sensed by those who cling to this position.

The supportive position is one that is extremely common and can be exercised in a very fatherly and feeling kind of way. Again, it is a position which has the priest stand on the outside and, in effect, deny what the person is really telling him. This is the way priests behave in movies when they say, "Don't worry. Things aren't as bad as you think." The easiest of all aphorisms, "What you have to do is to stop worrying about this," is a combination of the interpretive and supportive stance. There is hardly any phrase in the whole world that is more frustrating to someone who is in difficulty than this one. It means that the person really has not heard him, but that he has maintained a distance from which he can give off platitudes that are ultimately quite unhelpful.

This is the kind of position a priest can often assume when he is really vexed or feels helpless in the face of the tragic reality in which he finds himself. He does it because it seems like the only thing he can do. Yet he may be staying on the outside of a situation in which he could share much more simply and deeply, and thus provide genuine support. Why does he have to reassure others? It may well be because this is the only successful way he has of reassuring himself that he is effective, that he is a source of help for others. This is not to say that supportive remarks are never in order. We are talking here rather of a consistent attitude which enables us to remain on the outside of the real grief and struggle of people, whether it is in the midst of their mourning or in the midst of their marital difficulties, and not really participate in the struggle with them. It is quite destructive of really rich opportunities for personal sharing.

The probing attitude is not only common but it has acquired an immense instrumentation over the years. There are all kinds of elaborate report forms and questionnaires that are employed in dealing with the people who constitute the Church itself. The priest must ask himself once in a while, "What am I really finding out with all these questions?" It may be that he really is not getting any closer to the person with whom he is dealing. He may, in fact, insure that he will stay on the outside of the situation rather than penetrate the inner world of the other. It is a highly stylized way of relating to others.

Many times priests assume this viewpoint because, unless they could ask questions, they would not know what else to do. To ask a question, then, becomes a way of reassuring oneself that one is competent or effective in the pastoral role. But again it is to remain on the outside at a time when the real effort that the priest must make is to open himself to what the other individual is truly experiencing on the inside of his life. Questions may get at this at times but all too often the reward is to the questioner and not to the one questioned. This canonical style may make a priest's life quite dry and uninteresting because he becomes so preoccupied with getting dates and numbers and other information that he misses the opportunity for a deeper and richer relationship with those whom he serves.

All of these attitudes, and many of these overlap with one another, tend to keep the priest on the outside of his people. It is through the approach of understanding, which will be described in the next chapter, that a priest makes himself available in a full sense to the People of God.

Notes

1. Donald Weatherby, "Some Personality Correlates of Authoritarianism," *Journal of Social Psychology*, No. 64, 1964, pp. 161–167.
2. E. H. Porter, *An Introduction to Therapeutic Counseling* (Boston: Houghton Mifflin Co., 1950), p. 201.

8

The Priest Who Understands

At the end of John Rechy's agonizing novel, *City of Night,*[1] the tragic homosexual hero makes a desperate series of phone calls to various rectories in the city in which he is living. He is disappointed at the way in which his anguished effort at describing his problem goes unheard, or is treated unsympathetically, by a number of the priests he contacts. Finally, however, he pours out all his inner confusion to a priest who seems to sense what he is trying to communicate. Immediately a wave of relief sweeps over the miserable young man. Somebody else has understood, even for a few moments, the shadowy world in which he has felt so terribly afraid and lonely. The priest does little else for him but share in all his pain. Indeed there is little else that he can do for him but this is no small gift. It is the very thing that the young man has been searching for. It is what each one of us looks for but does not always find in moments of distress and trouble. Genuine understanding is the central attitude for the priest who would share in the lives of others at a deep level.

Almost unconsciously we tend to describe the people in our lives who are really able to help us as "very understanding." Those who fail to help us are described, again with unconscious accuracy, as "not understanding." We say of them "I just couldn't get through to him." These phrases catch the nub of human sharing that is so essential to personal growth. It is the individual who can put aside his own concerns and enter into our world for even a moment or two who manages to help us see ourselves more clearly and to possess ourselves more thoroughly. Without understanding, little communication is possible, and so the relationship cannot give life.

If pastoral relationships are to be marked by the gift of the person of the priest to the other, the priest must be skilled in understanding. He cannot pretend to do this because genuine understanding only takes place when there is authentic human interaction. There is probably nothing as frustrating for man as the experience of taking that desperate chance of exposing himself and his inner fears only to find that the other has not really heard or understood him. When a person pours out his grief and receives a platitude in response, he is genuinely dispirited. He may, in fact, become more defensive and less likely to share himself in the future.

It may be well to examine briefly the kind of goals that priests have in working with other human beings. If their aim is to effect a permanent and lasting change in others, a total cure, or a glorious happy ending in every life they enter, they may be doomed to great frustration. Christ himself did not solve every problem he met. Neither will the priest. Far more reasonable for the priest is to see himself as a source of growth for a person who is struggling to understand more deeply himself and his problems. He may not be able to cure the individual completely but he may contribute, through his sensitive understanding, to the strength and confidence the person needs to become more mature in his own life. This is not a trifling thing to do for anybody. For the priest it is the thing he can do for everybody. It is through understanding, a clear gift of the Spirit, that he can enter many lives and share at significant moments of agonizing struggle. He can thus help others to accept more responsibility for themselves and their own behavior.

Understanding is a way of describing the whole orientation of the pastoral worker. His mission is not to manipulate or force awkwardly constructed solutions on other people. He is called, however, to be open and receptive to them, to bear their burdens with them if he cannot take them away from them altogether. This is the vital aspect of pastoral work, this ability to enter the world of the other without losing one's self in it. It is what the American Indians meant when they spoke of "wearing someone else's moccasins." It is the experience touchingly described in *To Kill A Mockingbird*[2] as "wearing somebody else's skin for a while." The strength that comes to the other person when we truly understand him arises precisely because we retain our own identity and separateness from him and yet can enter his troubled and disordered world in a deeply sharing way. This calls for great sensitivity and great self-discipline on the part of the priest. It is one of the principal ways in which he can make his own person available to those with whom he works.

There are many misconceptions of what understanding

means. To some it seems a soft and irresolute commodity. To others it seems to be a diagnostic evaluation of the strength and weaknesses of the other. There are some things, however, which understanding definitely is not.

First of all, a truly understanding attitude is not agreement with the other person. Many people, when they seek out advice, flatter us in the process but also exert a certain pressure on us. They are not seeking our advice nearly as much as they are seeking our agreement. It is far more difficult to show people we understand their anxious desire to have our support than it is merely to agree with them and let them go their way. Understanding withstands the pressure of compliance in their wishes and gives the other something better and more lasting. It shows them that we sense exactly what they are trying to express. It shows a deep respect for our own person and for them. It is an extraordinary experience to find someone who takes us seriously. It does not seem to happen nearly often enough in life. A priest, of all professionals, must give witness to the world that he takes other human beings seriously enough to make the patient effort to understand them rather than just to say "Sure, sure, that's the way it is."

Understanding is not disagreement with the other. Both agreement and disagreement are a way of remaining on the outside, of making an evaluation from our point of view, and this is antithetical to genuine understanding. Disagreement is an easy response to give, especially when we feel secure in our own wisdom or like the feeling of giving advice to others. "No, you've got it all wrong," may allow us to exhibit our wisdom but it may also betray the fact that we have not really sensed what the other person is trying to share with us. It is an easy response, however it is not ordinarily a helpful one. The person whose habitual stance is to remain outside of other people and to evaluate by agreement or disagreement sometimes wonders why people go ahead and do something that contradicts his advice, or why they don't come back to see him again. It probably is because he has failed to enter fully the world of the other with sincere understanding.

In advocating understanding as an essential component of the pastoral orientation, we are not suggesting that there are no moments in which the priest quite properly makes judgments or evaluations. Understanding does not make him a blotter for all other human experience. There may be times when he must clearly reflect on his relationship with others and make some intervention which indicates his opinion in a particular situation. This may especially be true when he feels that the person with whom he is working needs referral to some other professional colleague, such as a psychologist or a psychiatrist. There is, however, a primacy for understanding even if one eventually must make these kinds of judgments.

Understanding is not a totally passive process. As we have indicated, this attitude is an active one, which enables the priest to give his whole person, his attention and his time, to the other. The emphasis in a relationship characterized by understanding is on the interaction between the two persons involved in it. The priest is not just the wall against which the troubled individual throws the muddy remnants of his life. His is an active presence and it is strenuous work for him to share deeply in the problems of the other. The emphasis is always on the total relationship and on the fact that the priest is not doing something to the other by way of manipulation. Nor is he focusing merely on the symptoms of the problems presented by the other. He is addressing his person to the person of the other. He demonstrates his willingness to try to achieve the internal frame of reference which enables him to see as if he were looking through the eyes of the other.

This requires him to understand and to express this understanding in some way that gets through to the other. It does not mean that he must rigidly refrain from healthy and spontaneous comments or any other kind of behavior that is genuine and that arises from his personal commitment to the other. It does mean, however, that the attitude of understanding is the foundation for the relationship. The priest is not an intruder in the privacy of another person, the all-knowing authority who hastily rearranges the psychological or spiritual state of the other. The priest is present, totally given to the relationship, in an effort to reach out in a human way and accompany the other through what may be the no man's land of his inner life.

Unfortunately, this kind of attitude is sometimes caricatured as placing the priest in a totally receptive role or in the position of someone who merely parrots back to the other person the statements that the other person has already made. These are superficial and insubstantial understandings of the matter. It is not the purpose of this book to give a detailed description of the techniques of pastoral counseling. These are readily available in many other works. It is

rather our purpose here to emphasize the attitudinal dispo-
sition of the priest who wishes genuinely to be effective in
assisting others to take fuller Christian responsibility for
their lives.

This viewpoint is incompatible with the authoritarian or
totally evaluative stance that enables the priest to remain an
external presence to other persons and to preach to them
from afar. We are discussing a basic Christian orientation
which demands an open quality on the part of the priest.
The priest involves and exposes his own self in relationship
to others. His willingness to do this is the absolute prerequisite for his effectiveness. This may be the psychological significance of Christ's words—

Then he said to him a third time, "Simon son of John, do you
love me?" Peter was upset that he asked him the third time,
"Do you love me?" and said, "Lord, you know everything; you
know I love you." Jesus said to him, "Feed my sheep.

> "I tell you most solemnly,
> when you were young
> you put on your own belt
> and walked where you liked;
> but when you grow old
> you will stretch out your hands,
> and somebody else will put a belt round you
> and take you where you would rather not go."
> (John 21:17–18)[3]

Here Christ may well be suggesting that the person who
is called to feed his sheep and to follow him will find that
his life will indeed be circumscribed by the needs of others.

Christ may be foretelling Peter's martyrdom on the cross as the Gospel writer tells us. He is also describing something of the given attitude that must mark the true pastor of persons.

The priest who is an agent of the Spirit constantly finds himself bound and led in ways in which he does not expect to go. The death he undergoes occurs in his efforts to share the burden of living with his people. He cannot command that their problems disappear and he cannot decide beforehand on some tidy and comfortable dimensions of pastoral work.

He must be responsive at every point of need in the lives of his people. This will lead the priest into situations and problems which he would not choose to enter except as the willing companion of those who are suffering these human difficulties. The priest dies a little in each relationship because he must yield something of his real self in trying to make the difficult journey of understanding with others.

This attitude of understanding demands that the priest work constantly at improving his sensitivity to others and at the development of the skills of counseling which will enable him to share life with others in a genuinely helpful way. The pastoral task for the priest, then, is not just to understand or categorize problems. It is not merely to achieve a diagnostic understanding so that he can affix a proper label to the behavior of others. His orientation will be to the persons who experience difficulties and to the depths and shallows of the worlds which they inhabit. As noted earlier, this is not a passive process but one that urges the priest to open himself ever more fully to catch accurately what others are trying to share with him. The next chapter will describe briefly some of the psychological principles involved in counseling built on the foundation of understanding that is truly a gift of the Spirit.

Notes

1. John Rechy, *City of Night* (New York: Grove Press, 1963).
2. Harper Lee, *To Kill A Mockingbird* (Phila.: Lippincott, 1960).
3. *The Jerusalem Bible* (New York: Doubleday & Co., Inc., 1966).

9

But How Do We Understand?

Our culture prides itself, at times, on its inability to communicate. It struggles with communication on a personal and global level and celebrates its disastrous failures in its black arts and politics. There is a Parkinsonian flavor to the increase in the medium and the decrease in the message. Everybody seems to be talking, singing wistful folk songs, or listening to assaulting transistor radios. And still the question remains: why should a process which should be so simple and for which such extraordinary instrumentation is now available be at once so complex and constantly frustrating?

Throughout the Church the desire for richer and fuller communication is expressed on every side. Priests and religious, having discovered their right to be persons, insist now on being communicated with in a genuinely personal way. They demand this, as the fixed postures that passed for life have fallen away and left them exposed to ponder the real values of being human. This is an experience many sensitive laymen have known for a long time. It was not only difficult for them to raise their voices but many in the Church questioned whether the laity had a right to open their mouths at all about the mysteries of Christianity and their role in the Church.

Many Bishops have tried to open up some kind of communicative dialogue with their priests and people only to find that it is far from a simple process. Effective communication is cited more than anything else as a first step in deepening the relationships of the persons who constitute the people of God. It is probably because communication was so stiffly formalized and channeled in earlier years that we were caught unprepared for the complexities that arise when human beings really want to talk to each other.

Genuine listening is not just listening to the words that a person speaks. Real communication is achieved when the whole message that the person is conveying, from every level of his being, is sensitively perceived and responded to by the person to whom it is directed. There is a redemptive quality in any interaction in which a person feels that he has really been heard by the other. This is true when a layman speaks to his priest and when a priest speaks to his bishop or even when the bishops together speak to the Pope. The crucial element is not simply that they get their way. They may be prepared for a refusal when they enter into dialogue with the other person. What is essential is that the substance of their communication is not blocked or turned aside or disregarded. If it is, they feel treated as something other than persons. Their frustration mounts and the harvest of enmities that goes with non-communication is reaped once more.

Most of us have learned some style of communication which has a built-in set of expectancies that have been derived from our previous experience. We have been through all this before, we say, as we listen to the dreary banter at a cocktail party. We have mastered the art of seeming to participate in the conversation we do not have to listen to. Sometimes we need not even speak since a judicious nod of the head, a few grunts, and an invitation to have another drink may carry one a long way in this social situation. We have learned to defend ourselves against communicating freely with everybody. This is a process which starts early and which is quite understandable. We do not tell the neighbors our business. Neither do we admit to every salesman that our mother is at home or give away freely to any inquirer the vital statistics of our life, our income potential, or our secret hopes and desires. Man must defend himself against a world constantly communicating with him in order to persuade him to buy this car, that cigarette, or this outboard motor.

Added to this, man does not communicate with other people to reveal what is wrong with himself. He likes to maintain at least a fairly respectable self-image. If it is at all possible, he will attempt to improve it in the eyes of others. In every normal person's life, there is a large quota of white lies, mild exaggeration, and carefully touched up reproductions of the past. There is a certain chemistry we work on our own personal histories that blots out what is ugly and painful while it adds gold to all the sunsets and blue to all the skies.

There is a whole range of needs related to our perception of ourselves that strongly affects what we see and hear in relationship to others. The man we describe as a pessimist, for example, immediately sees everything that can go wrong. The optimist, looking at the same situation, sees its bright promise and wants to move forward. What they see as they gaze at the scene reveals more about them than about what they are looking at. What was called the "new look" in perceptual research in psychology twenty years ago has pointed to the internal factors that affect so deeply our perception of the world around us. These same factors, then, also affect our communication since it is geared to what we perceive in the person and events of our lives.

We bring our life history to any relationship with another. We communicate far more of ourselves than we suspect to the individual who is sensitive and who can read the signs whether they are in our quivering hands or our strident tones. Man cannot not communicate. He communicates with all that he is, even when he is saying nothing or looking away. It is an extremely complex phenomenon, human communication, because it involves such deep levels of our being and occurs in so many forms other than verbal.

A large part of our difficulty in communication is that we have focused so exclusively on the verbal aspect of our interaction with others. The words, however, are sought and spoken only to express something of what we are experiencing in a more total fashion throughout our person. The words, when used by a Shakespeare, reflect all the fine shadings of human experience in a way that illumines and enriches us. Unfortunately not every man is a poet and the effort to translate what he feels into words that he can use effectively is quite arduous at times.

The words are only a part of the message and some of the

difficulty experienced in human communication arises from failing to realize this. Just as man is not merely intellect, so also what he expresses is not merely intellectual in content. Man is struggling to express the totality of his reaction in the face of his life experience. He strives to share his feelings about life and, as best he can, he attempts to compress these into words that he can speak so that another can understand him. These two levels, the intellectual and the emotional, merge together in human communication. Without a sensitization to the emotional level of human personality there will be no grasping of the full message that another is attempting to give to us.

The first lesson in understanding, general as it is, is that the priest must be open not only to verbal but to all forms of human communication. If he is really to understand the other it will not be in listening to *what* he says as much as it will be in listening to what *he* says. We are always trying to tell each other how we feel. We often phrase the question in exactly that fashion. "How do you feel about the war in Vietnam (or higher taxes, or the Democratic Party)?" This is not asking for cool intellectual appraisal as much as it is asking for where we stand in life. If we learn to mask this by comfortable phrases and cocktail party distractions, we sentence ourselves to an ever-increasing isolation from others. We cannot communicate unless we are ready to give something of ourselves away to the other, unless we are ready to share ourselves at some deep level with another person.

Understanding aims at sensing the total communication of the other person, the one that wells up through all the levels of his humanity and spills out through his glances, his moods, and his laughter as well as his words. This is where we find man, that most remarkable of creatures. He is not a recording with a flat smooth surface. He is a vital, distract-able, and sometimes elusive companion. He can charm and disgust us, thrill us or depress us, all within a few moments, when he is willing to open up the dimensions of his person-ality to us.

It is to this wide range of feeling that we must open our ears. The pastor cannot afford to be judged as one who has ears but does not hear. If this was a condemnation that Christ saw fit to make upon religious personages in Israel, it is one that could be made today on the person who is not willing to face what is involved in the process of communi-cation. It is a human activity and something of our own self always gets caught up in it. We cannot communicate with-out getting involved somehow with the other and this can at times be extremely threatening.

The root meaning of Christianity concerns people shar-ing life with one another. Life dries up and dies as people close themselves off in defensive worlds of their own. Life blooms when persons are willing to give something of them-selves away in each relationship they enter. They must be ready to change because communication often leads to this. This is also an upsetting prospect for some. They prefer to lead life from behind their more familiar and comfortable defenses which let but little of themselves out and, of course, nothing of anybody else in.

The focus for the person who wants to understand is not on diagnostic categories, and it cannot be on the preservation of himself inviolate in the exchange that communication demands. The pastor must focus on the total person of the other and open himself to the affective or feeling message that the person is trying to get across to him. This is what he must hear if he is to redeem the person through their sharing experience together. It is through this kind of sharing experience that the pastor and the other both grow in relationship to one another.

There is a mutual kind of sharing implied in any real communication and this must be the distinctive mark of all pastoral communication. The pastor hears the whole message and makes an effort to respond so that he can indicate that he has heard all that the person has struggled to tell him. This is basic to any counseling and psychotherapy only because it is basic to any kind of real human relationship. It is at the heart of the very intimate nature of the Christian pilgrimage of a people together. This is the significance of the presence which the priest can be in the lives of his people as they struggle to grow and give life to one another.

But just as Christianity is not tricks or manipulation, this kind of sharing must be deeply genuine if it is to be a hallmark of authentic Christian witness. There are many complications that follow even when we grasp this very basic notion of listening to the feeling level of the other. There are many mistakes that can be made even when one is earnestly trying to sense the emotional message that lies behind the intellectual words that are spoken. But this is the setting for real understanding. The pastor is challenged to put aside all the things that would keep him in the external frame of reference and to try to enter into the world of the other. This is accomplished when he can really open himself to all that the other person is in relationship to him.

The priest must strive to understand his own needs and his own defenses because these can so frequently block or distort communication. He must take these into account and be able to put them aside so that the message of the other is not distorted. He may well ask himself the question "What is this person feeling in order to say this to me?" This sets him in the right direction but this is a human process in which he himself is not left behind. So he must be prepared to face the consequences of being willing to communicate. He must be ready, in other words, to die to himself in order that his understanding may be fully alive. He dies to the defenses that have previously filtered out what others have tried to say. He dies to the fatigue that would have him put others off. He must be ready to die to the distractions which may flood his mind and carry him out of the present conversation. He must, in a word, come to life as a person himself if he is to be a person who even begins to understand.

10

Emotional Involvement

The very word "professional" has come to suggest in our culture an impersonal kind of relationship. It is frequently focused on the service performed in some transaction, be it legal or medical, rather than on the relationship of the persons so engaged. Wisdom has accumulated to demonstrate the fact that the doctor or lawyer who lets himself feel with his clients or patients will soon experience a shredding of his own emotional life. A professional relationship connotes some distance and reserve, a posture designed to prevent crippling involvements. The world is familiar with impersonal professionals who emphasize their service function rather than their personal presence for other pragmatic reasons as well. There is an endless supply of pressing cases and they must be managed through prudent husbanding of one's energy and financial resources.

The doctor-patient relationship has been one of the casualities of this somewhat defensive professionalization in the practice of medicine. The medical world is appropriately concerned about this situation and is actively taking steps to try to provide a remedy. Efforts are being made to sensitize doctors to the human factors in all illness and to develop the skills to respond to these as well as to heartbeats and blood pressures. Even industry has recognized that productivity and efficiency are closely linked to the kinds of personal relationships that are developed between managers and workers. The very heart of the pastoral relationship, of course, is that it must be personal or it is sterile and incapable of giving life.

The priest has not been immune to defensive professionalization. There has been such an increase in the demands for his service that he has naturally become subject to the same kind of pressures experienced by lawyers and doctors. For example, the priest called to minister to a large hospital will be hard pressed to do more than perform the service of distributing the Eucharist and managing with some decorum the last rites of the desperately ill. The pressure to see that these duties are fulfilled in a hospital with hundreds of patients automatically reduces the amount of time that the priest can spend with individuals. He may not speak to the sick at all and have little, if any, time to listen to them as he makes his rounds. I was struck by the scandalized reactions of a group of Protestant seminary students to what they witnessed of the pressured kind of pastoral care by priests in the large hospitals where they were receiving additional clinical training. They could not believe that pastoral care so stripped of any personal aspects could really represent the concern of Christ for his sick. It probably takes the viewpoint of somebody on the outside to make us realize how seriously impaired our ministry can be by the service demands that slowly but surely choke off the personal dimension in our work with the sick. This can be true in many other pastoral situations as well.

The enemy is not just time. It can also be the need to protect ourselves from entering into the grief and anxiety of all those who would want to share it with us. The pastoral figure sometimes develops a tough hide because he feels that he will be personally destroyed if he allows himself to become too involved in the internal life of others. This is a critical question in pastoral psychology. It is a realistic one because so many priests have learned their lessons the hard way through some previous experience of being severely hurt themselves through emotional involvement with others. They have decided that they cannot pay this price and still maintain any reasonably healthy function as a priest.

This is the consequence, often enough, of not having been helped to understand their own reactions and their own needs as human beings. It is no surprise to see that they may hedge the bets they make on sharing life with other people. They have been through it once or twice and have known the disturbed dreams and the anguish that arises when they have cared too much about an individual or a family. They have, perhaps, gotten too fond of a woman, and have suddenly found themselves absorbed and distracted by a relationship that has drained them of their energy and effectiveness. There are few priests, and these must be cold characters indeed, who do not bear the scars of emotional involvement with others.

It is no wonder that they have tended to back away and relate in a more impersonal and less exhausting manner.

The problem is, however, that the alternative to emotional involvement is not emotional isolation or defensiveness. The pastoral relationship dies when the person of the priest is withdrawn from it. The dangers of being willing to communicate on a feeling level with others are not effectively handled merely by trying to avoid the problems to which this may give rise.

The priest who honestly wants to understand and to share his person with his people must first learn to listen to himself. The pastoral figure must be able to sense what is going on within his own person, even when this is disturbing and difficult to accept. If he does not do that, if he does not open himself to his own emotional life, he has taken a step backward and will surely be controlled by his emotions even when he does not suspect it. This readiness to establish a sensitive relationship to one's self is basic to the good mental hygiene of priestly activity. It is the prerequisite for a man called to spend his life in establishing personal relationships. Unless he understands himself, he will surely lose himself, that is, lose clear focus on himself. He will then react to protect himself in the future from these murderous emotional involvements. The eventual high price that he will pay to defend himself against close relationships with others is gradual isolation from them.

This is why, in the era of clerical culture, so much personal investment of the self was made within the ranks of the priesthood. A man needed *some* friends with whom he could be himself, some stable associations to support him in a life that was potentially so emotionally exhausting. Many priests turned to hobbies and sports, not just to waste their time but to insure some healthy balance in their life when they felt that it was not only inadvisable but perhaps morally wrong for them to establish and possibly even enjoy close relationships with their people. Strangely enough, it is for these substitute activities that priests have received so much criticism.

Actually, many of these phenomena that have been classified as the luxuries of the clergy did not represent their wallowing in worldly excess at all. The good food, the long vacations and the large cars were the signs of men who were trying to solve a basic life problem. If they were not to be too dangerously close to their people, they had to put something in their lives to keep them from drying up or disintegrating altogether. They needed some personal satisfactions and, unfortunately, because human relationships seemed to be so dangerous, many of the things with which they filled their lives in the name of sublimation were really symbolic efforts to support their own emotional lives.

Thus, perhaps, the many evidences of high material need and expression in the lives of priests have arisen because custom seemed to put a ceiling on the possibilities of their psychological growth in relationship to others. Others represented danger. As a result the more normal course of psychological development through and in relationship to the people he served was dangerously limited for the priest. To put it another way, the consequences of this emphasis on defending himself against emotional involvement tended to keep him at a level where he had little choice but to make up for this lack of deep human relationships in ways which did not promote his full psychological development. I have often felt that this is why food and drink have always had such a significant place in the rituals of rectory and community life for priests. They were, in effect, responding to their emotional needs even when they did not realize it. This is an example of how one's feelings can control one in very complicated and subtle ways.

The feelings of loneliness that they might experience were really the cries of their inner selves looking for something better and richer, not just within the world of clerical culture, but within the world of their ministry to their people. These cries were too often stifled against the background of supposedly ascetic practices which constantly emphasized the dangers of the world and the safety and security of the priest in relationship to his brother priests or his community. His loneliness was to be "offered up" rather than explored and understood. It was often looked on as a weakness rather than the sign of his humanity's hungering for healthy relationships with others.

This is not, of course, to indict the whole world of relationship among priests. It is to say that healthy men are not only permitted but have a right to go one step further, to reach out into the world and share themselves in their work with others. This, in fact, is exactly what many priests have always done. Strangely enough, however, many of these have been thought rather odd at times because they were so deeply involved with other persons. They were breaking the code in some vague way and being disloyal to the fraternity in finding the center of gravity for their lives with their people instead of within the clerical world itself.

The Church no longer looks on the world as a menacing

environment. The priest is moving out of the confines of clerical culture and looking for closer and healthier associations with his people. It is all the more important, as this orientation becomes stronger, that the priest have a deep and thorough understanding of himself. It is quite possible, after all, for the priest to make all the mistakes that the previous defensive attitudes warned him about. He can move into the world of persons without really possessing himself completely and can soon find himself fragmented and destroyed precisely because of this lack of self-knowledge. This knowledge is not, however, merely intellectual. It is the fine tuning-in of the person on himself, not to become self-conscious or self-pitying, but to develop a respect and understanding of his own person, imperfect as he is, in relationship to others.

The priest must avoid the danger of a cold and removed professionalism because his emotional life will make demands that he will respond to in ways that he himself may not even recognize. On the other hand, he must avoid plunging himself headlong into the morass of human suffering without any understanding of his own needs, his own strengths and weaknesses as a human being. If he is to grow in relationship to others, he must open himself to the kind of man he is so that he will relate through what is real about himself rather than through what he may pretend to be real or wish to be real. The only thing he can really count on in human relationships is what is really there within his own person. This is not to accept failure or sin as much as it is to accept his participation in the human condition as a prerequisite for fuller growth. He must sense the whole range of his emotional life without feeling that this is some-how a weakness or in any way undesirable. He cannot be such a stranger to his feelings that he will be surprised by the complexity of those reactions that chiefly characterize the developing human person.

The priest must be ready to look deeply and forgivingly into himself and not demand the impossible kind of perfect behavior which we have described in an earlier chapter. In fact, the healthiest thing he can do is to examine the real nature of his desire to be perfect. It may not *all* be response to the Spirit. Some of it may be a response to the need to impress or overwhelm others, a subtle but pervading desire to be respected and applauded by them. One of the feelings most common among priests is a desire to be liked by other people. If one takes a look at this, one can easily see what a strong ingredient this can be in pulling a person toward one certain set of activities which would confer upon him the rewards of being liked. It would also keep him away from the whole range of activities which might result in his not being liked.

Many priests who study counseling discover that this dimension of "liking to be liked" has far more influence on their lives than they ever expected. As one of them said to me, after a long but fruitful counseling examination of him-self, "I never realized just how much my own feelings were pulling me even when I thought I was doing things for oth-ers. What I was really looking for, and it is still hard to admit it in a way, is for everybody to like me. As a result, I always did the things that made me popular. At the same time, I always found good reasons for not doing the things that might have made me unpopular. I stayed away from ecumenical activity, for example. I was always afraid the minister and rabbi in our town would kind of look down on me and I would be, you know, uncomfortable with them. So I was always too busy to meet with them and always cancelling engagements with them. The real reason, I think now, was that I was afraid of them and I guess I was afraid of seeing my own fear until I took a good look at myself. I thought I was free but I was really fooling myself all the while. I don't think I was fooling them, though."

This is a telling example of how this very simple and common tendency can markedly effect the direction and extent of a priest's apostolate. It is not a terrible thing for him to discover that a desire for popularity can exercise a strong hold over him. It is terrible for him *not* to discover it, and to lead a life in which he never comes to terms with himself in this way. The examples of this type of emotional domination of a person by factors which he will not allow himself to look at are endless. These are not discussed, however, to criticize the priest as much as to try to explore the very direction in which he must look if he is truly to free himself for the pastoral role. This is the area where the priest must die to himself. These are the feelings that must be faced and put aside if he is to give the gift of himself with any kind of integrity to the other. It is no easy task, this surrender of one's defenses, but it is the redemptive act of reconciliation to self that brings the priest to his own personal resurrection.

The real danger for the priest lies not in relating deeply with other people but in giving himself blindly and without an understanding of his own motivations. Many priests who have suffered the agonies of emotional involvement have done so, not because they truly cared so much for the other, but because there was such a large investment of their own need involved in the relationship in the first place. This element of their own need went unrecognized. That is why they became trapped in a painful and frequently non-redemptive type of suffering. The priest who decides, for example, that this married couple should stay together because he himself would be so disappointed if they separated from one another may find that his own need is the strongest determinant of everything he does in working with them. That is why, at times, a priest can feel so intensely disappointed when people make decisions other than the ones which he thinks are best for them. Priests have experienced bitterness because they really have not tried to free others as much as they have tried to incorporate them as agents of satisfaction within *their own* need-system. The priest who subtly seeks himself ends up, like the unfortunate man in the Gospel, losing himself.

The important point here is that this non-redemptive suffering is not necessary. The priest need not stand aloof from others. In fact, he cannot if he hopes to have a healthy priesthood at all. When he is willing to explore himself, to move into the darkness of his own needs and impulses, he will discover the true person he is. He will then be able to move much more easily and freely within the lives of others. He will be much freer in giving himself without permitting his needs to be the decisive dynamics in the relationship. This is something that requires growth and development.

The priest will not achieve maturity except in relationship to others and this demands that he move toward the real values of life instead of toward substitute values and second-best satisfactions. He can do this if he is willing to take a hard and steady look at himself and at his whole orientation toward others in his pastoral work. He will truly be redemptive when he can grasp his own inner-self, take account of it in the relationship, and enter it fully sensitive to all the factors that may play upon him during the course of it. His real danger lies in not understanding himself. At this point emotional involvement of a very destructive sort ensues. It is what breeds cynicism and a hard-shelled impersonalism. These are the very death of the nature of Christian ministry. It is no easy task for any man to understand himself and to be able to forgive himself for what he finds in his own being. But this is the task for the man who wants to be close to people and who wants his death in relationship to them to be redemptive instead of self-defeating.

11

Games Priests Play

The reflections of this book center on the psychological attitudes of the person who participates in the pastoral activity of the Church. In this chapter we will reflect on the essential quality of openness as well as on some of the concrete expressions of the closed attitudes discussed in previous chapters.

The first mark of the mature person is an open attitude toward himself. He is not constricted in his understanding of himself nor is he dominated by any need to see himself in a preconceived way. He does not sacrifice authenticity for pretense. He lives in relationship to others from what really is inside himself. This openness relieves him of the need to deny or distort his inner experience. He can literally be himself because he is under no pressure in his own eyes to be anyone else.

This openness is a basic quality that enables him to continue growing toward a real fulfillment of his own possibilities. He can accept himself, take account of his limitations, set reasonable goals, and move toward them without anxiety. He is not surprised by any reaction that may occur within himself and, instead of using some defense such as rationalization to explain it away, he can enter into it and seek with great integrity the source of it. The process of growth for a person with this orientation never ends. If it is challenging, it is also constantly enriching. This kind of person possesses himself and is able to love himself in a fundamentally healthy way. As a consequence he has something to share with others.

That is why we describe mature persons as "disarming." Because they do not employ defenses as the basis of their relationship with others, people automatically lower their own defenses in response to them. Mature persons do not feel that they must prove themselves and so they experience great freedom and healthy self-confidence in the whole range of their relationships with others.

This open quality is necessary if an individual is truly to become an instrument of the Holy Spirit. It is his openness to self and to others that makes his own person sensitive to the action of the Spirit. When he is open in this unself-conscious way he can truly be the source of the Spirit through his relationships with others. When a man refuses to be open with himself he closes off the Spirit and its effect on his life and work. This closure of the self to the Spirit perhaps describes in psychological terms what it means to be sinful. The sinner, some have suggested, is the person who refuses to grow up. He clings to an undeveloped life style which numbs him to the Spirit and other people alike. That is why it is so essential for the priest to face himself without fear and to understand that his growth as a man moved by the Spirit flows from this willingness to give up the defenses that lock him within himself.

With this developing openness to the self, the priest notices other changes occurring in his attitudes. He is able to accept himself and his imperfections more readily and to move with greater freedom and greater responsibility in the lives of other people. He is less judgmental of them, less moved by prejudice, and more able to see them as individuals rather than as stereotypes. Probably the most frequently reported reaction by priests to the experience of the study of counseling is approximated by this sense of growing openness toward themselves and others. They find that they are less afraid of themselves and their own feelings and that there is a new freedom which enables them to give more of themselves in their service to other people. With this freedom comes a far richer life for themselves. They begin to see people less as threatening and faceless masses and more as individuals with whom they can relate warmly and closely. They are able to put aside many of the techniques they have previously used in dealing with others. No longer is there a need to strain in order to "achieve rapport." These priests give up gradually and with great relief many of the games that they felt they had to play in relationship to their people.

Priests have a right to a rich and happy life in relationship to their people. They have a right to something better than conventionalized and carefully controlled modes of meeting and dealing with them. When they can be open to themselves, they find that they are more spontaneous, more loving, and more responsible in a healthy way as ministers of the Gospel. These are the characteristics that mark the lives of healthy priests. It is unfortunate that such an elaborate set of games developed in the name of a defensive and fear-ridden piety that is incompatible with the pastoral relationship.

To cite some of these games is not one more game, or merely to be called a sharply critical observer. It is rather to try to understand how these games develop quite naturally in the lives of men who feel that they must live at a distance from other persons.

1. The "Laughing Boy" game. This describes the affable, good guy priest whose chief response in almost every situation is laughter. This is not the laughter of joy but the reaction of a man so much on the surface of things that he is forced to make a joke even when this is the least appropriate response imaginable. Therapists who have worked with priests have often commented on the tendency of some of them to block their own self-examination by continuously laughing off their behavior or by some need to make nervous jokes at every turn. There is no doubt some inner-effort to reassure the self at the base of this kind of game. It enables the priest to stay at a distance from others by always cushioning his relationship with this dreadful and unhealthy kind of gaiety.

2. The "Parasite" game. This kind of game puts the priest in relationship to his people so that he can reap the rewards of their presence in his life while they get very little in return from him. There are unfortunately priests who are quite accomplished at this game and who are able to settle for the cheap rewards that it yields. They are forever wangling tickets for sports events, invitations to dinner, or the pleasant glow that comes from association with the rich or

the influential. It is a failure as a game because its rewards are ultimately empty and because it gives rise to such resentment among the people who are forced to play it with them. There is something very narcissistic in this way of relating to a world which must respond to "Father" and his needs at all times.

3. The "Expert" game. In this life style the priest operates by knowing all the answers for others' problems. He knows just what they should do whether it is a question of their life work, their sex life, or any and every decision of consequence. If the priest knows everything, he need not open himself to learn anything in his relationships with others. Gratefully, this tribe has diminished in the atmosphere of renewal where a new mood of uncertainty has settled into the lives of many priests. The very fact that ambiguity and uncertainty can be so disconcerting to many priests illustrates how strong was their previous need to be experts and right in all matters.

4. The "I Need to Cure You" game. This is closely related to the "Expert" game but it is played largely within the person of the priest himself. It occurs when he is unable to face and accept his own limitations or to understand that Christianity does not demand instant perfection as much as constant growth. This priest expects to succeed, according to the goals he has set, in every situation. He is deeply upset, and even remorseful at times, when he has not carried off some situation with the perfection that he demands in all his behavior.

This is a very self-defeating game because he cannot win it. He will never cure everybody, solve every difficulty, heal every wound, or convert every passer-by, any more (as we noted above) than did Christ himself. This unrealistic goal arises when he has a basically unrealistic image of himself. As his image becomes more realistic, so too will the demands he makes upon himself. It will be enough to help people take the first step toward growing for themselves. The reasons for this compulsion to cure lie within the priest's own personality and not within the Gospel. This is a loser's game and the priest who insists on playing it will end up in a very disappointed and discouraged state.

5. The "Projection" game. Here again the source of the game lies within the priest's own emotional life. When he is unable to face his own feelings and identify them correctly he may turn to the defense mechanism known as projection. He will find his own faults in everybody around him and will be able to criticize them safely because, after all, they are not really his faults but those of others. It is in this game that the strong hostility that priests can at times feel toward themselves is frequently expressed. Unable to accept and like themselves in any way, they rename their self-irritation as righteous indignation toward the sinners that surround them. They are long on harangue and short on compassion. It is a very self-serving device because it expresses his own inner feelings and attitudes in a way that deflects attention from the priest himself. This kind of anger is not really zeal and, in the end, it is a very isolating defense, precluding one's own genuine growth.

6. The "Let's Talk About It" game. This style of ministry is marked by flight into intellectual and excessively theoretical Christianity. The subjects of this game are more

often theology and liturgy but psychology and sociology often serve just as well. It is built on the premise that if the priest talks about these subjects he has really done something about them. That is why there are so many discussion groups on the subject of Christian love. It is far safer to talk about it than to give the gift of one's own imperfect self in genuinely trying to love some other person. This is a dangerous and tiresome game which quickly alienates people who are anxious to hear the words of eternal life and who are deeply unsatisfied with the tortured talk that often substitutes for this. Sex is often a victim of this kind of intellectualizing. Some of the archest commentary on the subject arises from people who are most deeply defended against the sexual component of their own personalities. This is the game that comes replete with catch-words, "in" jokes, and superficial scholarship. It is a refuge for those who keep their distance from life by talking about it.

7. The "Love Them and Leave Them" game. This game has gotten a lot of play in the age of renewal because it is related to the personalistic emphasis of our times. It is a game a man can get into when he is manipulating other people to satisfy his own needs. In many ways it is a combination of several of the games mentioned before. The priest can be both parasite and intellectualizer as he moves into the lives of others on a deep personal level and then drops them when the going gets rough. This is all too frequently seen in this age when many priests feel that some experimentation is needed in their relationship with women. They look on women as a means to the end of identifying themselves as full-blooded male persons. This reflects the fre-

quently described uneasiness of American men about their virility, but that does not excuse or justify it as a model for the relationships of priests with anybody. At heart, this is cold and calculating manipulation of others for the sake of the self. It has little regard for the other and this is quite evident when the priest beats a hasty retreat at the moment when things get too hot for him. It is so easy for him to justify this maneuver, on the grounds of preserving himself and his priesthood, without ever confronting himself and the feelings that led him into this kind of behavior in the first place. At the same time it is a rejection of an opportunity to grow and to work through in a responsible manner his relationship to the other.

There are variations on these games, of course, and most of us have played one or more of them at one time or another. The important thing is to be able to look at ourselves and see if we think that life really is a game or whether we have a Christian sense of values that reveals life as something sacred, to be lived with responsibility.

Irresponsibility for the person of others is one of the most common difficulties hindering the *aggiornamento*. It is so easy to speak of the great ideals of Christian love and personalism and to reduce them to a defensive game in our own lives. This is not only hurtful to others but it is also suicidal for the priest himself. The great discovery that the maturing priest makes is that he need not play any games at all in life.

It is strange that honesty with oneself has been so undervalued. This is probably because the life style of the priest has been so circumscribed by fears and controls whose effects were at least as bad and befuddling as the dangers they were supposed to remove. These games arose in a clerical culture when men were not allowed to feel free to bring their real selves into relationship with others precisely *in and through* their priesthood. The rules of these games were devised in an age when rules rather than the values of real life were thought to be of paramount importance. They represent the outcome of unchristian notions about the nature of man and his sharing in the life of the Spirit which we call love.

This defensive structure is crumbling away and the person of the priest himself is exposed as the most important instrument in his ministry to the human family. This requires a great deal of openness to himself and the kind of honesty and responsibility in living through relationships with others which once caused people to say of the Christians "See how they love one another." The priest must be a strong (if imperfect) man who is capable of living with his people in a richly sharing way. This is the only way in which he can provide the personal presence that is the heart of the formation of the Christian community around him. The Christian community only arises in relationship to him and this is impossible if all he has to offer his people is gamesmanship.

This genuine personal presence is also the only style of life in which the priest can truly grow and be effective as a human person and as an agent of the Spirit. That is why there is a psychological difficulty of real magnitude built into the efforts to describe the priesthood as a *function* rather than as a *profession* in the broadest sense of the

word. To accept the priesthood as a function is to endorse
the notion that ministry to the people of God can be accomplished successfully on a part-time basis. There is a
certain attractiveness to this thought but there may be
something of a game involved in it as well. The priest who
is not able to develop an image of himself as given fully to
his people will obviously identify himself principally with
some other task or occupation. His sense of ministering to
his people will be diminished exactly in proportion to the
attenuation of his identification as a full-time priest. Those
who propose this emphasis on function and occasional ministry have failed to understand the lessons of psychology
that tell us that truly productive persons in any field are
those who are able to identify themselves in an integrated
way with the societal role that they choose.

A sometime priest will have great difficulty in being any
kind of a priest at all. It may suffice to have this kind of
priest if all we expect from him is the celebration of the
Eucharist and the administration of the sacraments. The
Christian community, however, expects more from the
priest and from his humanity. It looks for a presence that
gives life to the functions he performs in relationship to his
people. The person of the priest who is to be the vital source
of the Spirit that will unite his people around him is still the
essential ingredient for the building of the Christian community. The chief resource of the priest is his own personality and it will be exceedingly difficult for him to utilize this
unless he can see himself as a *priestly* person, consistent
and wholehearted, from morning till night.

The priest who is able to face and accept his own personality is the free man who is slave to neither outdated controls nor superficial games. He gives these up when he finds himself. This is the truth, infused by the Spirit, the truth that makes him and his people free.

12

Renewal in Relationships

The true Christian does not play games with life. His attitude toward the world is one of constantly growing openness. This quality of openness is not a bland or vague one. It is the presentation of our true and imperfect selves in an undefended manner to other persons. It does not mean that we are some kind of free-flowing protoplasm that takes its shape only from what it encounters in its environment. This openness is found, in fact, only in well defined personalities who are nonetheless capable of entering into and sharing life with other people. Openness is not a product of wide-eyed and inexperienced innocence as much as it is the fruit of the real if at times trembling embrace of life in all its complexity and abrasiveness.

Openness does not come overnight. It develops as we respond to the prompting of the Spirit and this is sometimes a long and difficult process. It comes only to the individual who is willing to make himself vulnerable to all the hurts that can come to those who truly love. Because it is a vital process, it is never completed. Once a person surrenders to the Spirit, opening himself to others, he is continually challenged to give more of himself to them. The

Christian gives himself to others and through and in this process he finds his relationship with the *other*, the only source that can ever fill him. God is never far away for those persons who try to respond to the Spirit of love. That is why the real Christian does not need to play games.

The thirteenth chapter of First Corinthians is still a good description of the Christian who makes room for other people in the inner precincts of himself. He learns, with a great tender feeling for his struggling brothers, to be patient and kind and unambitious. He is not puffed up because he has learned how to empty himself even as the undefended Christ did in redeeming mankind. His aim is not to manipulate or persuade as much as to accept and understand.

When he gives himself over to this attitude, the signs of the work of the Spirit are also present in his life. These are the very things that modern men seek so desperately through the deceptive anesthetics of drugs and alcohol. The open person is at peace but he is no stranger to pain. The loving person experiences joy because he knows how to share sorrow. The Christian who gives up gamesmanship finds that life, like the good measure of the Gospel, is poured overflowing into his lap.

Any genuine renewal in the Church must go deeper than a refashioning of structures or a reworking of the formulae of worship. It is the relationship of man to himself and to his brother that must be renewed. The path to this is still through death to the old and defensive man who would keep us in cold isolation from the human family. Man must be reconciled, not just to a set of intellectual moral principles, but to his own being as a person. Through his own personality he must reconcile himself with other men. This is the change of heart that the voices of real prophets have called for through the ages. Without an awareness of the psychological realities of the human situation, it is a goal that is quite impossible to achieve. It is not too much to say that the renewal of the Church will safely follow once we have committed ourselves fully to the task of renewing ourselves through our personal relationships.

The servants of the People of God are called to be agents of just this kind of renewal. They are meant to bring the gifts of the Spirit to the human family, to help man find peace for himself and the world. This demands a thorough presence of the manhood and womanhood of all those who are called to serve the People of God in a pastoral way. The whole person and the whole life of the priest or religious must be given over to this ancient but constantly fresh challenge.

It is because those who share in the pastoral ministry of the Church must be so deeply involved at every level of their personality that it is dangerous to reduce their roles to the performance of certain sets of functions or to think that much can be accomplished on a part-time basis. If, indeed, one cannot see the total immersion of personhood that is required in patiently trying to develop this openness to the Spirit in the whole Christian community, then one is justified in asking why there should be priests or religious at all. I am not criticizing those who have placed these somewhat startling questions before our consciousness in recent years. They are good questions because they make us search deeply in ourselves for answers which can justify lives given totally

to pastoral caring for the Church. The person who participates in this pastoral charge must bring this vision of Christian love to life in his total and full-time orientation to
mankind or there is not justification for his giving all of
himself or herself to the task.

It is because the life and work of so many priests and religious have been reduced to performing certain functions
while living at a distance from others that these pointed
questions have been placed before us. That is why, if the
priest is called to be nothing more than a good Christian,
one could challenge the concept of full-time priests. This
also explains why so many religious can ask "What makes
me different from anybody else who might be doing this
same work, whether it be teaching, nursing, or social welfare?" The difference only arises when their whole person is
absorbed in making the Christian understanding of human
sharing available to other men. This is impossible unless
they see that their witness is incarnated in the models of
thoroughgoing loving relationships they are meant to provide for others.

The priest or religious must be Christians *par excellence*,
the catalytic agents in the development of the Christian
community. This community will not automatically form
itself. It is their instrumentality that provides the core
around which Christians can build their relationship to each
other. To develop identifiable Christian communities which
represent the reality of persons who share the life of the
Spirit and the nourishment of the liturgy and the sacraments together demands the presence of servants whose
whole lives are committed to this task. While this presence

is essential for the development of centers or parishes as places of worship and education, it is also essential for the growth of the community members in personal relationship with one another. The pastoral figure becomes the servant person whose own openness and surrender to the Spirit offers, as Paul offered to his communities, a model for the Christian's relationship to God and to his brothers.

The pastoral figure is a locus of Christian relationship even as the altar is a locus of Christian worship. The priest and religious share the pastoral responsibility of the social reality of the local Church. Without their pastoral presence there might well be worship but it is difficult to imagine that any stable community would exist. Questions about priestly identity and religious vocation have arisen because the once appropriate cultural forms of relationship to God's people are now disintegrating. These previous forms highlighted the priest's function, especially his cultic one, while providing him with a mode of relationship which kept him at some presumably proper distance from his people. So too, the religious was there to teach or to perform some other function, but his or her life was primarily oriented to the religious rather than the larger pastoral community of the Church.

The priest and religious lived stylized existences which were described to them as "ways of perfection." The gradual over-emphasis on this separatist ideal closed them off from the world rather than opened them to it. There was little vision communicated to them that unified their lives and activities for the sake of the Christian community. Their "way of perfection" tended to isolate them from anything

like an intimate sharing with this Christian community.
The value of Catholic education, for example, has been
questioned because it was not seen sufficiently as an integral
part of the pastoral response of the Church. Religious were
seldom allowed to develop some sense of their teaching
apostolate as an essential part of the development of the
Christian community that is the Church.

At this time, however, many priests and religious have
learned that life that does not flow from genuine relationships with others is hardly life at all. As a result, previous
somewhat restrictive forms of the apostolate are becoming
less attractive. The previous models presented them with a
life of their own which was lived in parallel but separate
fashion from the rest of the Christian community. This
style of distanced life is now sharply questioned because it
seems to drain away the very meaning of life itself.

An interesting illustration of this is found in the evidence
of the sensitivity sessions which have become so popular
with priests and religious in this country. Sensitivity sessions, originally designed to broaden communication in the
business world, aim at helping an individual enter more
deeply into himself and to uncover the obstacles or defenses
that keep him from expressing himself more deeply and
honestly with others. When these sessions are supervised
by competent professionals, they can be extremely helpful
in opening life up in a very rich and basic way to the par-
ticipants. The striking thing about the priests and religious
who sometimes enter these groups is their frequent report
that this is their first genuine experience both of themselves
and of what it means to trust and be trusted by others. That

is one of the reasons that these sessions have become so popular.

The enthusiasm of religious for basic encounter groups has made them something of a fad in the Catholic world in recent months. The message in this is, of course, that something must have been radically wrong with the kind of "life of perfection" they were presumably living before they entered these groups. They ache with the realization that they had become adroit at playing games with people, at staying on the surface of life and never really even knowing those with whom they lived and worked closely. I think there is an incredible indictment of the former conventionalized forms of priestly and religious life in the results that are coming from these experiences.

It is not unlike the discovery many religious are making, now that some of the rules of their life have been relaxed. For example, some religious who had been isolated from each other at meals through public reading and the observance of silence most of the time have encountered real problems now that these restrictions have been relaxed. Now that there is nobody reading to them and more opportunity for conversation, they are suddenly confronted with getting to know each other. This has caused surprising anxiety in many of these situations. Life was far easier, despite the archaic regulations, when one did not have to open oneself in relationship to other persons.

This terrible spreading discovery of how lonely they have been for so many years makes many religious question whether their community life ever had very much meaning at all. By disastrous evolutionary process, some communities had become, not settings where people freely shared life together, so much as arrangements that enabled people to live together without knowing each other. There is a terrible thirst for closer relationships with other people in the lives of many priests and religious at this time. All this suggests again that the basic renewal that is required is one that centers on human relationships rather than revised rules or structures.

It is because the human deprivation has been so great in this now dissolving form of clerical and religious culture that many question whether they can continue in a life in which they have lost faith. This is, of course, to mistake the accidents for what should be the substance of priestly and religious life. The only substance that is Christian indicates that renewal for the Church must offer its servants the opportunities for truly human lives. Any community or diocese that does not make it possible for its members to serve mankind in a close and loving way has already written its own epitaph.

The present difficulty is intensified because the realization of the need for this radical renewal is very slow in coming. A terrible price is paid by the Church when it cannot provide the condition of a dedicated life in which someone can be truly human and loving while at the same time he or she serves the People of God as a priest or religious. The price is paid in those who feel they must leave what they conceive to be the "institutional Church" in order to find circumstances of life in which they can be truly Christian. That means that they have discovered a new set of values, far closer to the Gospel, as they see it, than their rule ever was. Yet there seems no room for them within the structures through which they had tried to give their lives for the People of God. There is a double price paid in this situation. The religious orders and the priesthood lose members who are vitally needed to carry on the work of helping men to understand the real meaning of Christ's message of love. At the same time, many of those priests and religious who separate themselves from the forms that seem to stifle them find a new loneliness and isolation in the world outside the institutional Church.

Many of these have felt that they could serve the Church just as well by teaching school, working for the poor, or engaging in some other activity on their own. Yet something important is lost when they can no longer identify themselves as part of the pastoral presence that the institutional Church should truly incarnate in this world. They no longer feel that they are sharing in bringing the good news to other men because, in their experimental communities or their lives on their own, many lose a sense of sharing in the corporate response of the Church itself. They are no longer perceived by others as part of the ministering response of the visible Church to the needs of the world. They are seen and admired as highly responsible Christian individuals. For many, however, this is not the same as sharing in something that can be recognized by others as the saving mystery of the corporate Church itself.

What is needed at the present time is a rehabilitation of the concept of an institutional Church. This latter phrase has taken on unpleasant connotations because it conjures up a vision of impersonal bureaucracy, an ecclesiastical machine where priests and religious are disposable parts. The Church cannot, however, shed its public institutional character and still manifest itself as a sign of a loving people who share life together. The sign is fragmented and contradicts itself unless it can present a thoroughly human institutional presence in the world. These concepts are by no means incompatible. The challenge, spoken to the Church both from within and from without, is not to abandon but to renew its institutional character.

This renewal can only be achieved if adequate attention is given to the Church as a community whose vigor depends on the openness of the personal relationships of its members. There can be no room for a class of servants who live a separated life, supposedly justified by higher goals of sanctity. The People of God are called to the same holiness through sharing the life of the Spirit together. Priests and religious are called to live their lives in and for this community. Without their committed full-time pastoral caring for their fellow Christians, the development of a healthier institutional Church is impossible.

For this reason, the Church must provide ways of life for its servants which do not separate but rather link them intimately with all other men. Unless renewal includes this understanding of human relationships as essential to the building up of the whole Church, there will be a continuing loss in the numbers of those needed to minister to mankind in truly redemptive fashion. Only refashioned forms of priestly and religious life which center on close relationship to the total Christian community will guarantee a saving corporate presence for the Church in this world.

The institution of the Church must allow itself to be transformed, not to destroy itself, but to discover a new heart to revivify its pastoral presence. Reconciliation rather than renunciation is the need of the institutional Church, a reconciliation which provides room and opportunity for service to all those anxious to give all of themselves for the sake of all—for whom Christ died.

13

The Theologizing Person

Man lives, whether he perceives it or not, in a redeemed world. He has, as his main task, the discovery of who he is. As Karl Rahner has observed, he is "a being who is only in the process of discovering what his being is. He is a being open toward the infinite . . ."[1] The struggle for his identity will only be completed in God, but this only emphasizes the importance of the patient search for the self in this world.

Fantastically disguised and sometimes grotesquely expressed, man's struggle to find himself is displayed across the market and meeting places of every culture. The priest has a special charge to listen carefully to man's communications, to sense the meanings of his signs and diversions, to catch the human longings beneath his contradictions and confusions. He must first attune himself to the many-timbred voices of the human family. For everywhere, whether at peace or war, at rest or leisure, the pulse of mens' anxious search for fulfillment can be felt.

A zoologist can look at man, call him the "naked ape," and persuade us of our animal qualities. A poet senses something of man's spirit and translates it, sometimes in a half-blind way, into brittle couplets or flowing rhythms that reflect his own personal engagement with life. But the Christian, and particularly the priest, must be able to see all of this and more about man. The priest, if he has the ears to hear and the eyes to see, can understand man, beneath his many disguises and half-grown postures, as God's creature trying to find himself and to make his way back to the Creator. He must discern the great potential of the human person in a world that is more than a cosmic accident.

The task for the man or woman who lives by the Spirit is to understand the redeemed world, and to point beyond the struggles of the human race to their meaning in view of theological reality. The person who would carry out the pastoral office must reveal to men the full truth of life. It is more than a drama for sophisticated apes destined for a climax in the death of the sun a billion years from now. It is the story of human persons, touched and enlivened by the Spirit, called to become more intensely human as they move, as individuals and as a race, towards God. The true priest shares in man's struggle to be more human, revealing in his own person the growing fullness of life that comes to those who live by the transforming power of the Spirit.

Those priests who see their role as the watchmen of the human family are frustrated when men persist in being less than perfect. Those who believe that their task is to solve all mankind's problems suffer the frustration of all earthly utopians. Those who feel they can minister to man from distant ivory towers cast themselves in an equally unrealistic and ineffective role. All these miss the meaning of life as a steadily evolving but always incomplete process. The priest serves growing and imperfect men who are more often than not unaware or unsure of their own promise and their true destiny. The Church is a presence that is a sign of God's relationship to man. It is the home, not for angels or the self-righteous, but for sinners who are trying to find themselves. The ministry of the word must become flesh in the lives of those ministers who are ready to share in mankind's agonies, and to illumine them with their own vision of God's universe.

The great mediating role for the priest is to share the truth of revelation about life, to celebrate the life of the Spirit sacramentally, to translate the good news of redemption in deeply human terms. He must be a theologizing person, not as one who contemplates truth in his study, but as one who deals with the meaning of life in the light of theology in the anxious presence of mankind itself. The pastor need not have the answers but he must disclose himself as struggling with his brothers to find them.

The theologizing person does not speak neat and ultimate expressions of divine revelation that purport to immediately clear away the mists. He does set himself to express more fully, in changing conditions and cultures, the truth of revelation as it applies to any and every problem mankind faces. This is a struggle and places him right at the joint of time between the secular and the sacred. The theologizing person constantly tries to reveal the meaning of life by his open reflection on it. He does not present man with a pre-recorded litany of theological aphorisms. His theologizing is live, done in the company of those who suffer and long for more than the husks of contemporary despair. It is the presentation of his own person, not as the complete expert, but as the individual who applies the hopeful truths of revelation to the suffocating array of modern problems.

If there is an answer to the serious questions about what makes the compassionate priest, nun, brother different from the compassionate social worker, psychologist, or psychiatrist, it comes from the theological dimension which they bring to their work with other men. Father Charles A. Curran compares the pastoral relationship to familiar Dutch paintings.[2] In these, the scene of family gathering or human work is set frequently against a background where a window opens out to a broader landscape of the world beyond. In the same way, the pastoral relationship, even when it is focused sharply on a particular immediate problem, always opens up to the context of the redeemed order of creation which is its true setting.

This added dimension does not supplant the needed counseling skills of the priest in relationship to his people. It is not the mindless insertion of pseudotheological pieties which awkwardly invoke the supernatural. It is not the honeyed reassurances that God will provide or that God's will must be done, blandly mouthed in the face of human failures. It is rather the dimension of belief that places the present human struggle into the context of the theological reality that is the setting of all life. The mature priest relates the problems of life through his own person to the revealed truth that alone illumines the human enigma. This is an active and perennial task, requiring a willingness to seek the fuller truths of theology in constantly evolving human situations. It is a public process that is not satisfied by recourse to principles or categories developed in more primitive stages in our understanding of God and man. It is a process that must be characterized by openness and questioning, study and reflection, as well as active sharing in the doubts of decent men.

Any area of human activity yields examples where this kind of theologizing is not only appropriate but urgently needed. Perhaps the most obvious recent question that illustrates this is birth-control. Something has clearly been out of phase in the relationship between theology and the world's honest concern about the meaning of marriage and the responsibility for population control. Theology, until recently, tended to remain static, seemingly content with its position regarding the ends of marriage and the significance of the natural law. But men of conscience questioned these absolute positions in the light of the pressing problems which affected not only individuals but the human race itself. The great lack of continuous theologizing in dialogue with the socially concerned disciplines tended to intensify rather than resolve the issues involved. The loss has been two-fold.

First of all, the Church seemed to many intelligent men who were trying to deal with the problems of population control to have pulled its royal robes more tightly around itself and to have looked away from the problems of the world. The Church seemed frozen in a posture of false security, like a statue that somehow survived in a city razed by bombing. Fancied or not, the Church did not seem ready even to hear the questions proposed to it by the human family.

Secondly, the Church suffered from its own lack of self-examination, from its own failure to reflect on its pastoral relationship with mankind. Its somewhat numb insistence on the totally changeless nature of the truths it had to share with the world prevented it from understanding that developing insights are not only possible but compatible with its role. This inflexibility has recently yielded, but only after the disease of irrelevance had become far advanced. The hurry to catch up, the sudden and dramatic readiness to open itself anew to the reality of the world around it, has disrupted the lives of many who had been taught to accept it as a serene and immutable teacher. Even while it struggles to speak intelligently to modern men, it discovers that they have proceeded with their own solutions and no longer care much what the Church decides. Within the Church its own members wonder what confidence they can now place in it as a teacher and guide.

This set of difficulties is familiar to everyone. The problem is to reestablish a truly pastoral relationship with the community of mankind. This can be accomplished only if the need for a constant and dynamic public theologizing over the real concerns of the world is realized. The Church must engender the atmosphere of freedom and trust in which this can take place. That means, of course, that it must provide the pastoral vision which its priests and people need in order to exercise this theologizing presence in the world. The task is not to cap the gusher of truth and to contain its explosive energy, but to enable it to be brought forth in all its richness for the welfare of the human race.

This process occurs in the lives of individuals who understand that this is not just an intellectual exercise. It is rather the total involvement of the pastor in the human situation. Here he patiently tries to understand the true nature of the varied problems and to respond to them as a man whose own values flow from his embrace of revealed truth. He struggles as a man of faith whose faith makes a difference in what he is like and in what he has to say about the difficulties of man. This is no easy task because it demands openness to both man and the Holy Spirit. But this is the essential characteristic of the theologizing person. He is a man growing in his own understanding of the mystery of redemption and he joins himself in helping his fellowmen find themselves and their own redemption in the struggles of their daily lives.

The theologizing person is much needed in a world deeply troubled by questions whose moral implications are not at all clear. He must stand by the statesman or the scientist and reflect with him on the implications of his decisions across a wide range of behaviors. Indeed the pastoral figure cannot abdicate this responsibility and leave these men without the theological viewpoint which their own milieu so often fails to provide for them.

The decisions about birth-control are a case in point. In effect, weighing moral issues as best they can, statesmen and scientists are making the practical decisions about population control. But who will speak for the whole human person, if the pastor refuses to relate his understanding of man to the difficult problems of the day? Man, as God's image fashioned for the life of the Spirit, is too important to be left only in the hands of scientists and statesmen. This is not to accuse them of moral insensitivity or some kind of ethically-blind pragmatism. It is to say that, insofar as their activities enlarge or delimit man, they need the voice of the theologizing person who can speak clearly of the Christian view of man. It may seem easier to let doctors or lawyers or senators struggle with their own consciences about their responsibilities toward man. It may be easier still to stand outside of their environment and to make judgments, fiery with wrath at times, about their mistakes. The pastoral figure, however, belongs along side of them, attuned to their doubts and concerns, a brother to them in their efforts to make morally informed decisions.

Doctors, for example, have many burdens placed on them in our day and have been asked to make a staggering assortment of judgments on man's behavior. They are already plagued with enough self-confessed ethical uncertainties about the beginning and ending of life. While they deal with the harrowing clinical realities of the problem, birth-control, for example, remains more than a medical concern. Dr. Spock notwithstanding, most physicians are uneasy about donning the mantle of philosopher or moral theologian.

It is not, after all, that we do not know enough about the physical side of family planning. Indeed, the emerging technology of conception control may soon by-pass and render meaningless the tired natural law discussion. The Church, when it theologizes about man in relationship to his invention, must place the question into a broader frame of human values.

The basic setting is that of human relationships and their Christian significance and potential for all mankind. We

whether one is hurting others or not? I am not suggesting that these questions cannot be answered. I am saying that they are difficult questions and demand more than a casual inspection of our motives. And what of the hippies who have made the Christian vocabulary their own? They don't want to hurt you, they say, but if they do, they are quick to reply "That's your problem." Love may have rich significance for those who use it in these contexts but quite often it does not. More frequently it is a convenient but insubstantial by-word that is unrelated to continuing responsibility in relation to others.

But what, deep down, do any of us seek in life, if not something more lasting than transient moments of intimacy, something more durable than irresponsible slogans? It is something that enables us to share life more deeply, something that relates us more fully to the human race as persons. Married people want to plumb the depths of personal sharing, for this is the very essence of their lives. They are not afraid of the redemptive character of genuine love. Husbands and wives need the nourishment of each other's total personality. Only this is the root of the faithfulness and hopefulness that nourish the sharing which outlasts the thousand fissures of every life. Loneliness and longing, these contemporary haunters of the human family, are not relieved except by that deepening gift of lovers to each other in sharing life as completely as possible.

Death is somehow involved in real loving, the death to defensive selfishness that brings resurrection and fuller life for those who give themselves earnestly in love. This is the inevitable Christian dynamic, the paradox obscured but not dissolved by the ages, the core truth of living by the Spirit. Lovers still find themselves only by losing themselves in each other, and this is what men need urgently to understand. The death undergone in loving has a spontaneous quality about it. Love is mechanized by the charts and thermometers of rhythm, which has made the word *sacrifice* taste somewhat sour even as husbands and wives pronounce it. But genuine love involves lovers in a steady yielding of their lives to each other in the whole pattern of their mutual devotion. Technology will not replace what is so deeply sown into the nature of love. Birth-control can only be seen in perspective by those who have entered into the meaning of Christian love. It can only be placed in this perspective by those willing to theologize before the face of struggling mankind.

There is a thread connecting the questions of birth-control and celibacy, the thread of life itself and the nature of love itself as a sharing in the Spirit. Both discussions are impoverished if they begin with legalisms or technology. Both questions necessarily confront us with what we believe about what makes us human, and thus instruments of the Spirit, in committing ourselves in love to anybody. These questions cannot be resolved by men foraging for love but only by those who understand something of the mystery of the love they would give. Only with a Christian sense of values about love can men speak with either freedom or conviction about the pressing issues of our age.

There are so many implications for the future existence and growth of mankind itself that churchmen dare not stand by and let scientists or politicians take up alone the human problems of our time. There is a wide range of difficulties from heart transplantation to city planning that needs the illumination of the Christian vision. Never was it more important for us to accept the Gospel charge of helping men to understand and experience the real meaning of love and its source in the Spirit. We cannot afford to speak in intellectual theological categories or as preachers on the far edges of the human situation. We must theologize in living words before the world of men, and this is no easy task. But it is our pastoral task, more clearly now than ever, or we will have misread the signs of the times, and forfeited our right to say anything at all to man.

Notes

1. Karl Rahner, *Theology for Renewal* (New York: Sheed & Ward, 1965), p. 83.
2. Charles A. Curran, "A Catholic Psychologist Looks at Pastoral Counseling," *Pastoral Psychology*, 10, February, 1959, pp. 21–28.
3. James Kavanaugh, *A Modern Priest Looks At His Outdated Church* (New York: Trident Press, 1967).
4. Paul Goodman, *Like A Conquered Province* (New York: Random House, 1967).
5. Margaret Mead, "The Life Cycle and Its Variations," *Daedalus*, Summer, 1967, p. 872. Reprinted with permission of *Daedalus*, Journal of the American Academy of Arts and Sciences, Boston, Mass., Summer, 1967, "Toward the Year 2000: Work in Progress."
6. Erik H. Erikson, *Insight and Responsibility* (New York: Norton, 1964), p. 132.

14

Calling the Church into Being

Philip Watson has suggested that the Sacraments of the Church stand guard against the overintellectualization of the Gospel.[1] We all run the risk of limiting the meaning of faith to an assent to neatly scored sets of propositions about God. That is why some renewal resembles the pretentious writing of modern film critics who delight in a new realism which, in many cases, is only the projection of the director's tortured inner world, a broken mirror in which man may see a thousand splintered reflections of only parts of himself.

The growing emphasis on personalism and on understanding the Church as a people who participate in the struggle of life together, demands that we focus on real life and on the ministry of the word that is made flesh in the relationship of the pastor to the community he calls together around him. The theologizing pastor does not preach only information about Christian beliefs. He calls the Christian community into being through the ministry of the word by making it sensitive to Christ's summons to life. This makes him a central figure, caught in the tension between two worlds, whose own person becomes a revelation of reconciliation to the Christian assembly.

The priest calls the Church together through a preaching that is fleshed out in his own understanding of his relationship to the community around him. This is a task not just for his intellect but for his whole personality. His own person becomes the focus, or core point, around which the community of Christians can gather as a people who live in the Spirit together.

To establish the Church the priest needs a sensitivity that transcends the intellectual so that he may understand the groups who already constitute, by their bonds of relationship, a human community. His task then becomes that of helping its members to discover a deeper richness of union in the Spirit and to nourish and celebrate this in the sacramental life. He has neither call nor need to dominate a community nor to lead it in some totally predetermined way. He is meant to be the principal source of the Spirit which allows people to establish deeper and more loving relationships with each other and to grow through these relationships to their fullness in Christ. The community of the Church is essentially pilgrim in nature. It radiates out, through its members, to the world around it. In this way it shares its own life to help other men find the fullness of themselves under the guidance of the Spirit. A priest is called, then, to assemble a community which celebrates not only itself but one which senses and celebrates its mission of priesthood to the whole human family.

The priest is meant to foster relationships among his people, to help them open themselves more fully to each other because of his own openness to the Spirit. His preaching cannot be a distant intellectual proclamation, but a human giving of himself and his faith to the community. Just as the final revelation of the Christian good news is found in the life of Christ, so continuing revelation comes through the person of the priest in the loving and defenseless presentation of himself to his people. That is why in *Ecclesiam Suam*, Paul VI could describe the modern apostolate as one of dialogue. This is not just an exchange of intellectual musings but an interpersonal experience of the most demanding kind.

The recent revolution in catechetics centers on an appreciation of the human dimensions of revelation in our day. Repeatedly in the Gospels we are struck by the fact that the Christian pilgrimage is described by Christ in terms, not just of intellectual commitment, but of self-discovery in relationship to others. Cadbury describes it in this way:

The kind of knowledge Jesus looked for was not so much imparted information as insight achieved. There is in fact reason to suppose that he did not refer so often to what His followers were to be told as to what they were to recognize and to discover . . . Jesus' complaint is that men do not recognize the implications of their attitudes.[2]

The minister is commissioned to recreate, to reincarnate insofar as he can, the quality of Christ's own relationship with others. This is a deeply human undertaking, marked by openness and a complete and unconditional acceptance of the other. This is storied throughout the Gospels whenever Christ meets someone; his way is not to dominate or threaten him, but to allow the other to find himself in their very encounter, to *experience* the truth that love is the summation of the law. The religious leader who does not see himself as a mediator of the personal relationships of his community, fails to be a mediator of revelation to that community. It is through his own humanity that the word of God must come to life and form community.

This will not happen merely because the priest tells people to love one another. It does not come about just because he designs structures to enable them to meet face to face or to discuss common problems. The priest exercises his priesthood in relationship to his people through his total personal presence. This becomes an effective agency in helping them to open themselves and thus find themselves in relationship to one another. The Spirit works through this human instrumentality to form the community around the priest. The identity of the priest and the meaning of his work become clearer as we reflect on the process of growth in the interpersonal virtues of faith, hope and love which the building of the Christian community entails.

The priest is, in this rich understanding of his ministry of the word, a builder of community, not through artificially contrived intimacies, but through the presentation of his person, enlivened by his commitment to the Gospels, to his people. This priesthood is not merely one of sacramental function but of personal interaction and constant interrelationship on all levels of life with those whom he serves. This, in fact, is the essential meaning of his vocation of service. He is the servant whose own style of life presents the model and the means by which other people open themselves to the promptings of the Spirit in relationship to one another.

It is already platitudinous to say that what is important is not what the priest does but what he is. The difficulty is that we have not plumbed the implications of this description very well as yet. He does not have to be a master social worker, nor a skilled psychologist, but he must make his own person available through all the relationships that are associated with his preaching of the Gospels. It is through this kind of ministry that he frees the priesthood of the faithful so that they can then build a Church in the world around them. This is the meaning of the Church. It is not just the work of the priest who settles for forming a community around himself. As said before, he is also the agent who opens his priestly people to their mission of sharing their love in the wider community of mankind.

There is no way to understand the priest except in relationship to the community of persons which surrounds him. The old confining clerical culture, though ineffective, is not yet dead. There is, in fact, a real danger that it will come to life again, with a changed face and a more subtle influence. This pseudo-renewal is a danger from which none of us is exempt. It is so easy for priests to think only in terms of their own needs and their own lives and to fail to see their priesthood in its relationship to the priesthood of the faithful. A priest who abdicates his own identity so that he becomes "just one of the faithful" has forsaken his charge to be an agent, a *minister*, in the difficult process of community building.

Thus, his task as a priest related to his people is not one

that can be absorbed into some more general meaning of the priesthood of the laity. His first work is, through his own human instrumentality, to build the Christian community so that it recognizes itself as such and understands and lives by the vital truths of the Gospel. Without the presence of the priest, who is freed from everything else so that he can accomplish this task, the Christian community has no rallying point or source of self-understanding. Unless his whole person is there at the very heart of the gathering of God's people, the Christian community lacks the mediator who is meant to be its source of life and truth. That is why, despairing of finding priests with some sense of their role as community builders, so many Christians have withdrawn from the contemporary parish or have sought some underground or extra-territorial ground for sharing the life of the Spirit together. The Church fragments or becomes a sluggish and amorphous mass when the priest fails to understand himself as the man chosen to be the center of the Christian community.

In his role as the builder of community, then, the priest must recognize that the faithful exercise their priesthood in a way that is different from his. They exercise it in the world around them. It is his work to help them understand this as their calling and to help them find their source of energy and support in the Christian community which he calls into being. The new clericalism tempts the priest to make his community members over into priests in exactly the same way that he is himself. This is to fail to understand the differing gifts of the Spirit that are meant to flower in a truly Christian community. It is also to reveal the remnants of clerical categorizing that cannot understand the life and mission of others except in terms of its own experience.

This is exactly what happens when the priest emphasizes too much the inner life of the Christian community for itself alone. When he loses sight of the fact that the Christian community comes together in order to go forth in varied ways to serve the needs of the world, the priest has shrunken the horizons of salvation so that they fit within the measurements of his own world. When he fails to understand that his must be an open personal presence to his people so that they can become an open presence to all of mankind, he is likely to close them off in a self-centered, self-contained ambit of Christian practice.

That is why, at times, some priests have so intensively emphasized the Cursillo Movement or the use of sensitivity sessions within their own flocks. The clerical mentality becomes obsessive with us and we tend to seal our people off, rather than open them up to the world. The Church is only called into being, however, when it is a community whose priest helps its members to discover themselves in relationship to each other and to find and exercise their priesthood in relationship to the whole world. This is how the Church is built, this is how its saving presence as a people of God is revealed to the world. The Christian community turned in on itself lacks a sense of mission. Until it develops this understanding of its loving vocation, it is simply not a mature Christian community.

The role of the pastor is central in developing these widening circles that represent the Church as servant to the world. We need a broadened understanding of the meaning

of the pastoral figure. Surely the People of God, through
their priesthood to all mankind, share in the pastoral responsibility of the Church. This is generated in them through the
pastoral activity of the priest. It is difficult for him to exercise this or to claim this as his exclusive right. It is important
to see that the needs of the community and the limitations
of individual priests demand the development of teams to
share his task of building community.

It is time, for example, to recognize that the priest works
in relationship to the men and women who serve the Church
as religious brothers and sisters. In fact, unless he is the central figure in a team which reflects the nature of the broader
Church itself, it is difficult to imagine that he will ever help
his community members come to an awareness of their own
share in the commission to bring the good news of the
Gospel to other men. The priest may be a key figure in a pastoral team but he is not the whole team. He needs the support of co-workers who understand the pastoral dimensions
of their own task of teaching and allied work as essentially
related to the building up of the Christian community. One
cannot isolate the various contributions of priests, sisters,
and brothers from one another without diminishing the
potential that they represent in working together. There are
good theoretical and practical reasons for this need.

First of all, the pastoral team incorporates the men and
women who are servants of the Church in relationships of
trust and sharing which demand a high degree of Christian
commitment in their work together. Their inter-relationships
are a source of strength for one another and a constant re-
minder that their lives and work take on meaning only inso-

far as they are helping their people to form or find a community of relationship around them. The relationships of the pastoral team, then, serve as the model of self-sacrificing faith, hope, and love which translate the word *witness* into living terms no man can ignore. When the people sense that a pastoral team works together for their sake, they begin to understand what the message of the Gospel is all about. The members of the pastoral team reveal something of the quality of relationships that are possible when individuals do give themselves over to the workings of the Spirit.

Perhaps this will never be embodied perfectly in any team. However, the pattern of relationships among the members of a pastoral team who are struggling to grow more open and truly Christian in relationship to one another presents to others a realistic example of what human relationships illumined by the Spirit can be like. Priests, sisters, and brothers working together participate in the vocation of the pastoral leader. They not only support each other in the work and offer a model of Christian relationship to their people but their lives should be an effective symbolic answer to the suffocating atmosphere of alienation and estrangement which so plagues modern man.

The difficulty in the past has often been that the various servants of the Church have seemed to be in competition with one another rather than persons called to cooperate with one another. Everything tended to emphasize their separation and distance. This made it difficult, of course, for them to sense that their fundamental commitment was to share in the ministry of the word which, in its interpersonal dimension, makes a reality of Christian community. The golden age of clerical culture tended to separate them from each other and from their people and to focus excessively on their own lives of perfection according to rules which often had little relationship to the genuine struggles of life. The world of action for priests and religious lies not in dramatic new apostolates that further isolate them from one another. Life begins when they learn to share life with each other in order to bring the Church into being around them.

Clericalism still asserts itself, however. Many priests feel that their primary obligation in charity is to create a community of fellowship *with their brother priests*. This same thing is reflected in some of the supposedly innovative experiments of religious groups which still center on creating a form of life that is to be shared only by the community members. These efforts contradict the essential meaning of the Church itself. These further obscure our understanding of the pastoral vocation which priests and religious share together.

There are many difficulties involved in committing ourselves to a concept like the pastoral team. One need not demand that everyone be called to this kind of work. But unless a substantial portion of the Church's servants realize that their lives are to be given together for the service of the Church rather than to the observance of some rule or the preservation of some clerical cultural form of life, there will be very little headway made in calling the Church into being.

The world deserves something better from us than this. We are expected to love it and to love it unto the end. The priest, in relationship to his co-workers in the apostolate, can call the Church into existence even before he has a building or a home of his own. He can do it whenever he cares to, whenever he senses the deeply personal nature of his vocation to help people find each other in and through relationship with him. His pastoral care is exercised for this community in order that it may discover its own measure of priesthood and bring this in turn to the world. The pastoral responsibility is shared by the priest with his co-workers in the pastoral team. All these relationships, guided by the Spirit, are ordered to calling the Church into being.

Notes

1. Philip Watson, *The Concept of Grace* (London: The Epworth Press, 1959), p. 27.
2. Henry J. Cadbury, *Jesus, What Manner of Man?* (New York: The Macmillan Co., 1947), pp. 94–95.

15

The Setting of Redemption

The process of renewal in the Church, untidy and ill tempered at times, has revealed a polarity of positions about growth in the life of the Spirit which resembles many other contemporary discussions. It reminds one of the long-term debate between those psychologists who emphasize genetic inheritance and others who underscore learning as the explanation for man's behavior. It smacks of the tension between the camps of psychiatrists, one of which finds the origins of mental illness in organic causes and the other which prefers functional or non-organic explanations. It is not unlike the theoretical physicists divided as to the wave or the particle theory.

Within the Church some emphasize strongly the primacy of man's relationship to God and a love which is to be given to him alone. For them, life is a somewhat stark ascetic pilgrimage into the desert away from the campfires of human involvement. The recent emphasis on personalism inspires others to find this view as too unrelieved and inhuman. These latter say that although the Christian life may be filled with deserts, these deserts are in turn filled with people. For them God is not found in isolation but only in and through relationship with other people.

No one approach in any of these discussions corners the market on the truth. Perhaps a deeper wisdom will some day show us that they are not necessarily incompatible. In any case, the Christian always finds himself on the border line of these perhaps arbitrarily delineated worlds, called to live in the tension which demands an openness to God and to man at the same time.

What does this Christian life look like? Christ seemed to demand that we relate these worlds to each other. "But the world must be shown that I love the Father and do exactly as he commands." (John 14:31) How indeed is the world shown the effects of grace? What are the correlates in our experience for the processes of reconciliation and redemption which are such central themes in the Scriptures? What does the man who has been converted to God look like in relationship to his neighbor?

If the process of redemption is extended in time through the Church, then the pastoral significance of each Christian life must be revealed in its human style of response to other men. "We for our part have crossed over from death to life; this we know, because we love our brothers." (1 John 3:14) The Scriptures urge us constantly to reproduce the redemptive characteristics of Christ's life in our own. "Live in love as Christ loved you, and gave himself up on your behalf as an offering and sacrifice." (Ephesians 5:2) The Christian life is incarnate, as Christ's was, and if its source of energy is the Spirit, its expression must be in an active and saving love toward one's neighbor. If Christ's life is the model of the way we are to relate to others, then whenever we truly love we are sharing in the redemption of the human family. "It is by this that we know what love is, that Christ laid down his life for us and we in turn are bound to lay down our lives for others." (1 John 3:16)

The emphasis in the past certainly said that men first must establish a relationship with God which would then serve as foundation in their relationship with their fellow men. This connects God and neighbor but in a consequent rather than a correlative way. Men sense at this time that these processes are not and cannot be independent in time or experience from one another. There is one setting for life and that is in the community of mankind. The Spirit touches us not in isolation from men but whenever we are open humanly through our efforts to reach out in understanding and love to them.

Men cannot successfully divide themselves and really participate in the life of the Spirit. As we have noted earlier, the failure to recognize man as a unified being has given rise to unworkable models of human personality. But the Spirit does not touch only man's soul, any more than the world touches only man's body. It is unified man breathed upon by the Spirit who lives in the very heart of the family of man. Man's turning to God, his reconciliation with him, does not demand a turning away from other men and the world. The processes are intimately related. Man cannot live by the Spirit unless he strives to live in open and loving relationships with his fellow men. The Spirit is not available to those who close themselves off from the human condition and try to live as angels.

It is important to understand the human setting of the continuing process of redemption. If it is not to be found in flight from the world, then it is expressed across the whole range of human relationships. This is where the Spirit finds man and provides him with the grace he needs to share himself with his neighbor. If we are to find where redemption takes place in life, then we must find out where life itself is lived. There is no other place where we can locate the action of Christ in redeeming the world except in and through our relationships with other people. Father Charles A. Curran lights up the way for us in a brilliant article in which he explores many of the great themes of revelation and illustrates their meaning in and through pastoral relationships. Having described the counselor as one who incarnates himself in a deeply sharing way with the troubled person, he goes on to say:

From this incarnate process of self-exploration, evaluation and growing integration, the client or patient increasingly becomes aware of his own meaning as a person. By such slow and often painful self-acceptance, he comes to participate in his own redemption. In striving to understand and accept his total self, he becomes increasingly "whole." His redemption depended on another but it was also due to himself. Without the therapist he could not have arrived at this, yet it is not the achievement of the therapist alone. The person himself has literally "fought a good fight," and achieved this through his own efforts—granting that the therapist's gift of himself was necessary to make this possible. Thus redemption follows upon incarnation.[1]

Redemption is a shared process, one related to the human community, rather than to the breast-beating sinner all alone in the desert. It is when an individual is accepted and understood by another that he can begin to "find himself" in the very rich meaning that this phrase has in the Gospels. It is in a profound and trusting relationship with another that the sinner can "take on the body of a man," that he can truly become himself.

Redemption does not involve, then, merely man in relationship to God. The Spirit is made available to us when, as sinners, we are accepted and understood by those who have time to open themselves in real love to us. What saves us is what we are to each other under the breath of the Spirit. It is not the haranguing of the cold and distant preacher that brings redemption. This approach, already sufficiently indicted by the world's rejection of it, breeds fear and an infantile religious posture which makes man a cowering child in the face of a tyrannical father, God. But "there is no fear in love" (1 John 4:18) and there is no fear in the life experiences of trust and sharing that are the only things of value in men's pilgrimage together.

Those who redeem others through reaching out in love to them must first die, in a very real sense, to themselves. They are crucified with Christ because they have "put off the old man" who is blind and deaf to the needs of his brother. They lower the defenses that make them settle for a selfish and self-defeating isolation from others. Alienation and cynicism are the bitter fruits of fear-laden and defensive human relationships. The gifts of the Spirit, however, mark the lives of those who open themselves and expose their own imperfection in order to reach out lovingly to others. Crucifixion awaits any redeemer, a crucifixion that occurs in the context of his relationship with others. It is the surrender of his own person, in pain and yet in peace, that is truly redemptive.

We reach God because other people come into our lives who are truly living by the Spirit. These are the real givers of life, the ones who make reconciliation with God possible because they help us to reconcile ourselves to ourselves. They help us to love ourselves in a truly accepting and realistic fashion. It is here that the stage is set for the Spirit to come and fill us with life.

Thornton remarks about this process in the conversion of St. Augustine:

The way was prepared for divine-human encounter by Ambrose and Simplicianus. Ambrose offered Augustine a relationship "not as a teacher of the truth (which I utterly despaired of in the Church), but as a person kind toward myself." Simplicianus, like Ambrose, gave Augustine a warm, personal relationship. He listened to him. He participated in Augustine's defiance and doubt, trusting this to prepare further the way for repentance and faith.[2]

The pastoral figure is called to offer a model of this kind of redemptive relationship to his people, to foster within them the openness that will enable them to exercise their special priesthood throughout the range of relationships that fill their own lives. This is, in the human condition, an imperfect and gradual process. This, however, is the face of redemption in this world. It is not all lightning conversions and untroubled happy endings. The Christian life is a continued growth in loving, a constant and ever deepening sharing of the real values of life as they are illumined by the Holy Spirit.

Redemption takes place when men forgive each other for their failures and their sins, for their forgetfulness and their blindness. They can only truly do this through the power of the Spirit which reaches them in the heart of their human struggles with each other. Redemption takes place, as noted earlier, in the relationship of a husband and wife who understand that growth and love demand a constant reaching out in sensitive understanding to one another. Redemption occurs between parents and children who are not defeated by the slogans of the generation gap or by the complexities of their changing relationship with each other. Children are redeemed when parents take the time to look beneath their defiance and seeming alienation to see the struggling and growing human persons who are truly there. Redemption takes place whenever we open ourselves, and thus die to our own selfishness, to hear fully what another person has to say. We thereby understand who the other person really is and help to make him whole. These are the relationships that are grounded in faith and hope and love, not as frosty theological abstractions, but as experiences in the Spirit that take place between persons in life itself.

Redemption takes place whenever one person is willing to assume a real loving responsibility for another. This is not the responsibility that seeks to control or dominate. It is rather the responsibility that dies to the temptation of manipulation and reaches out to love the other and "to love him to the end." This kind of loving responsibility does not take flight in time of danger, as did the hireling in the Gospel story. It is more like the shepherding presence which faces the dangers of life with the other, and with a faith which truly makes the other person whole.

This is the responsibility for the other which enables married persons to remain faithful, not merely by avoiding sin, but through a willingness to live up to their commitment to each other even though life changes them and their circumstances. When a person loves responsibly he shows the world that there is another answer to the complex problems of civilization than "dropping out." He does not reject false values and then run away from them. Instead, under the Spirit, he patiently tries to understand and transform the lives of those around him.

This kind of responsible personhood which recreates the redemptive cycle of Christ's life is the very gift which the Christian community can share with all of mankind. It is the secret resource of Christianity that can recreate the face of the earth even at this darkening time in history. This is the only force that can be pitted against the grinding and seemingly blind economic and technological gradients which relentlessly re-create the face of the earth in an inhuman way. This quality of life will be more needed than ever in the angular geometry of the new world that is rising around man at this very moment.

In human relationships, only Christian love arising from the Spirit can heal the illness of the human spirit which so many social critics have commented on recently. This is what makes salvation available at any moment, the fact that there is a Christian community led by the Spirit to care for man in his struggles in a contrary and threatening world. If there is hope to be given to mankind, it must be done in a truly human and loving fashion. This is the whole meaning of the Church's presence in the world. There is no other place for redemption to occur and no other source for it but ourselves, imperfect and struggling though we may be. This is the miracle and meaning of Christianity.

Notes

1. Charles A. Curran, "Toward a Theology of Human Belonging," *The Journal of Religion and Health*, April, 1965, pp. 235–236.
2. Edward E. Thornton, *Theology and Pastoral Counseling* (Englewood Cliffs, N.J.: Prentice Hall, Inc., 1964), p. 99.

16

The Cold War Is Over

Years ago General DeGaulle told the West that it had already won the cold war and that it was time to turn the
focus away from the tension between Communism and
freedom, toward the development of other new sets of economic and political relationships. Within the Church the
cold war is also over. It is now time to shift the focus from
the-old-Church-versus-the-new to the development of a genuine sense of responsibility among the People of God who
constitute the post-conciliar Church. The important victories have been won, the age of transformation is well advanced. We can put away the old battle flags, retire the
old villains and face the reality that many observers have
sensed as already present.

The huge difficulty in this transition reflects McLuhan's
thesis that people do not recognize the future even when
they are living in it. In *The Medium Is the Massage* he
writes:

The past went that-a-way. When faced with a totally new
situation, we tend always to attach ourselves to the objects, to
the flavor of the most recent past. We look at the present

through a rear-view mirror. We march backwards into the future. Suburbia lives imaginatively in bonanza-land.[1]

This rear-view style of life is reflected in assorted documents of the renewal. It is even obviously present in some of the documents of Vatican II where the hopeful phrases for the future are found intermingled with echoes from a dead past. Many of the declarations of reform and renewal address themselves to and merely redress the grievances of an age that is already over. This is understandable and human but it puts true reformers at a disadvantage. They are constantly waiting for something spectacular to occur, some bell to ring or trumpet to sound, which will proclaim that the new age has finally dawned. Instead, seasons have changed, as they always do, quite gradually. The second spring is indeed here, even though there may still be a skim of ice on the river and patches of snow on the shady folds of the hills. Renewal is, in its essence, as irreversible a process as springtime. The clock cannot and will not be turned back.

It may be helpful to review some of the victories, if one cares to style them that, which have been achieved. The authoritarian style of Church administration, which was the very soul of clerical culture, is no longer effective. It does not work and the desperate efforts to reassert it have only hastened its complete eclipse. Unfortunately, some have observed the failure of authoritarian style and too quickly and simply have labeled it a crisis of obedience. Collegiality, despite the strain and tension associated with its development, is the very spirit of the day. The overwhelming majority of sensitive churchmen and churchwomen who are conscious of their responsibilities have already laid the groundwork for developing the models that reflect this commitment to consensus. These steps, awkward and wandering at times, have been in a forward direction. They can never be retraced.

Within the ranks of the laity, clergy, and religious a number of movements have emerged which have gained in momentum only over the past few years. Notable are the parish and diocesan councils as well as the senates and associations of priests. Groups of religious have worked diligently on a wide variety of projects which reflect not disobedience but deep loyalty to the Church as a saving presence in the world. Experimentation is widespread and increasing every day. This represents a shift of the center of gravity in the operation of the Church. The Bishops and religious superiors of the Church can no longer function effectively without an understanding of this significant change.

There have, of course, been excesses in the process of renewal. Many mistakes have been made, rude things have been said, and ever cruder phenomena have appeared in the name of greater freedom and responsibility for the members of the Church. These excesses, however, do not mar or discredit the basic principles on which renewal is based. Although many adolescent expressions that pass for apostolic zeal are embarrassing, they are at least mistakes made by people who are trying to head in the right direction.

Perhaps the best comparison, if one were to survey other human processes, would be the unfortunate excesses of which the labor unions have frequently been guilty in their great struggles to win basic rights for working men. It would take a long time before the unions could commit enough faults to even approximate the injustices committed against the common man during the era of the robber barons. So too, it will be a long time before the mistakes made in the name of renewal will even approach the mistakes and crimes committed by those who substituted an authoritarian style of administration for the healthy exercise of authority within the Church. We can tolerate the excesses of the present, not merely because they do not nearly equal the opposite excesses of the past, but because there is a dynamic self-correcting process at the heart of mature renewal efforts. This tends to correct abuses without sacrificing the positive spirit of advance which may have contributed to their occurrence in the first place.

The point of all this is that the age of collegiality is present for all those who are prepared to take a share of responsibility for making the Church come alive at this time in the world. The great danger lies in fighting the old battles, in failing to understand that they are largely won, thus failing to grasp what is truly occurring in the present. There will not be any single splendid event to mark the change of season in the Church. Those who wait in the wings for cues for their entrance on the stage of renewal have already missed the most important part of the drama.

The real crisis of the present is not one of authority and obedience. There are too many people deeply loyal to the Church and committed to the needs of mankind to sustain that thesis. They are not trying to escape work, although they may be yearning for more effective methods and structures to carry it out. So too, there are too many religious superiors and bishops who understand the needs of the Church to imagine that their only concern is to preserve ineffective authoritarian modes of governing it.

The genuine crisis of the times is that of responsibility. It is not enough to sing the impassioned songs of freedom, or to damn the failings of the past. The day of salvation is at hand. The most compelling difficulty resides in those priests and religious who maintain a passive stance at a time when they should actively assume responsibility for the pastoral presence of the Church. There is an inverse paternalism involved in this, a demand that the bishops and superiors perform magical feats to solve all the renewal problems. This is, of course, impossible. Some people in authority who are anxious to develop collegiality in their diocese or religious community are frustrated because not enough of their personnel are willing to step forward and assume their share of responsibility for it. This is not to deny the recalcitrance and intransigence of some religious leaders. It is, however, to recognize that there are significant numbers of those in authority who are open to the spirit of the age and who will in no way prevent their personnel from moving forward if they really want to. The question is: do they want to? Or are they waiting for pilgrim stars or other wonders to guide them?

A new Church is forming itself around those men and women who can open themselves to the Spirit. The Spirit is leading them to give their lives fully for the sake of a Church that offers men community with a social awareness that transcends mere companionship. It offers them courage

enough to follow the Spirit even through desert places, and
the comfort that arises from a confidence in themselves that
transcends a snug passivity in the face of uncontrollable and
shifting destinies. The leadership of the Church is already
in the hands of these people because it is only in and through
their presence of service that Christ's Church is really alive
in the world. They may live within the transforming structures of a Church where authoritarian minds still misunderstand them and authoritarian voices can still censure them.
They are, however, the Church that is alive and growing,
the Church they are working so hard to build that they fail
to understand it has already come into being.

These people cannot afford to misunderstand the measure of their success. The Church of tomorrow is alive today
in the priests and people who are accepting their responsibility for its saving presence. Their chief danger lies in their
failure to recognize this and the subsequent danger that
they may invest unwarranted amounts of energy in battles
that constitute, in effect, overkill of the past.

The hang-up in many situations is on the part of priests
and religious who have not really broken out of their docile
attitudes, despite their noisy complaints about Church
leadership. They can take their healthy share of leadership
any time they are willing to give up their dreams of a para-
dise that will be created for them from on high. The new
Church does not come into being, nor should it, merely
from the top down. Priests and religious may have to fight
still for their share in their Church in some places. In many
others, however, the conditions, although not completely
perfect, are sufficiently open for them to move forward any

time they feel strong enough for the task. They do not have to repeat the arguments of the past. The demands of the future are too pressing for them to head into it with their eyes fastened on their rear-view mirrors.

There is evidence that the most sensitive members of already existing renewal structures understand that the future is already here. They understand that it is time to move outward, away from their own concerns, toward assuming broader responsibility for the pastoral presence of the Church. Priests' senates and associations, once they get past the accomplishment of goals that center only on the life of the priest (personnel boards, retirement policies), must put all their energies into vitalizing the priesthood as an instrumentality of service to the People of God. No bishops will prevent them from doing things for the Church in this positive way.

In the same way underground parishes, which may initially have provided a medium of worship appropriate to the needs of their members, must come into the sunlight. They are at the point of turning outward to share their insights about community building with the rest of the Church. Failing to understand this, they can only turn inward and their joy will soon evaporate if their sharing remains their secret. They contradict the very meaning of Christianity itself if they cannot move beyond the stage of meeting merely their own needs. Hopefully, this is exactly the stage many of these communities have reached. The next responsible step is outward where they can lose nothing in giving the gift of themselves and their experience to others.

This is the same problem for many Catholic journalists. They have been eloquent in their indictments of the past, in tumbling down the false gods of blind authoritarianism. Now it is time to cease their exercises in sensationalism and to assume responsibility for positive growth of the Church in the present.

Religious communities of women have cleared away a good part of the forest of incidental concerns about dress and schedules and have focused on new forms of giving their lives in service to the Church. The new religious woman is already here, and she is here to stay. She needs the support of all fellow Christians in her continued efforts to move forward. Recent events have only made this fact more clear. Those who are trying to pull nuns back into the past have really only underscored the amount of growth that has taken place. They have, much against their own intentions, guaranteed the progress of sisters into the future.

The cold war is at an end, despite the explosions on the horizons. They are only on the horizons. It is time to let the dead bury the dead. Contemporary Christian living demands responsibility more than recriminations, the fulfillment of promise rather than the repetition of protest. It is difficult, as redemptive life in Christ always is, but it is the authentic sign of the times, and we cannot afford to misread it.

"To everything there is a season," the author of Ecclesiastes tells us, "and a time to every purpose under heaven . . . A time to kill, and a time to heal; a time to break down and a time to build up" (Eccl. 3:1, 3). Renewal has its seasons. The time to break down outmoded structures is now yielding to that most fruitful of times, that in which to build, and it is already upon us.

Notes

1. Marshall McLuhan and Quentin Fiore, *The Medium Is the Massage* (New York: Bantam Books, 1967), unnumbered pages.

17

A Community Casebook

Building the Christian community is a process that is marked with the redemptive signs of incarnation, death, and resurrection, as we have remarked before. The human task that confronts both priests and people invites them out of their separate worlds of loneliness, the one of clerical culture, the other of exclusively family-bound relationships. Neither of these worlds is big enough for the Christian who strives to give himself to the Spirit.

There is a variety of experimentation in the efforts to develop deeper communities in the Spirit. No two may follow the same plan or pattern, nor should they feel the need to do so. Nonetheless there are inevitable common features because the members of each group, in a genuinely human way, must deal with and work through the meaning of incarnation, death, and resurrection in relationship with one another.

Because there are common features, it may be useful to reflect on some of these in the experience of Christian community building which I have witnessed. Many of the observations in this chapter come from the members of Christian communities which have grown to the point of turning outward to share what they have learned with others.[1]

The members of a new Christian community generally find each other because they share a common impulse to live the life of the Spirit more deeply. They are striving to understand their own identity as Christians and are looking for means which will enable them to achieve this and express in a realistic way the intellectual convictions they have about being the Church. There are literally thousands of people who long for some situation in which they can share and live their Christianity at a deeper level than they now do. Dissatisfaction with parish life is not enough, nor pique at the tithing system, nor protest about the tactics of the pastor. Resentment is not sufficient motivation for the effort to find a place in a more intimate Christian community.

An important feature of these Christian communities which have grown up all through the United States is that they are not necessarily disruptive of parish or diocesan life. They are rather unique realizations of what can be done even now by people who are sincere and open enough to the Spirit to move forward in learning to share life in Christ together more fully. There is no contradiction with traditional Church policy. The Second Vatican Council has made it clear that the priest's position is close to his people and that his task is to bring them into community with one another under the Spirit. He can achieve this, even within the boundaries of the most traditional parish, and he can do it quite in the open. The new permissions for home liturgies further underscore the Church's own recognition of the fact that the parish can reach out in many different ways to nourish and support smaller communities within its boundaries.

These small groups have no rallying cry to destroy the old parish or to overturn the authority of either pastor or bishop. Instead Christians who move into this kind of community together are anxious to give their full vigor to the pastoral presence of the Church. There is nothing to be feared about these developing Christian communities. They have far more need of encouragement than of drastic authoritative control. As a matter of fact, they are probably the only sure sources of vitality, genuine wellsprings of the Spirit that enable the Church to come to life as a People of God in any environment.

It is important for the Christian community to maintain its perspective on its relationship to the parish and thus to the diocese. These are the normal and healthy channels which make these communities a vital part of the total People of God. This is the bloodstream, as it were, into which the communities' energies are poured for the building up of the whole Church as a people. Those Christian communities which fail to understand this, or which reject it outright, shut themselves off from the Church. They are not only diminished by this but they also diminish the whole Church insofar as they fail to contribute through their energies to its vitality.

In its essence, membership in a Christian community is a free response to the Spirit in which the individual seeks to understand his own gifts and to bring them forth to share them with others. The first experience, then, is incarnational since he chooses to deepen his commitment to the Spirit through deepening his commitment to the other persons who are members of the community. Incarnation is difficult because it demands self-revelation. This is the very thing that modern man finds so threatening. At the same time he hungers for sharing with others. Alienation and loneliness are the heavy prices he pays when he is unwilling or incapable of giving up the defenses that shut him off from other people.

The first act of a Christian community is one of trust, trust of each in all. This is a growing trust, the trust of beginners who will never get over being imperfect. It is especially at this initial stage that the presence of the pastoral figure is important. It is the pastoral person who can alert the Christian community to its vocation, not only by the word that he preaches, but by the way he complements this with the openness of his own personality, of his readiness for friendship and growth with others. Christians find themselves through their relationship of response to the person of the priest and others who willingly share the pastoral responsibility.

The priest's presence at the core of the Christian community may well give us our best insight into the meaning of his celibacy. It illustrates the fact that the gift of celibacy is not given to the pastoral person for himself but for the sake of the development of the Christian community around him. It is not given so that he may dominate others but so that he may, through his own person, unite others. I think that it is here, in trying to comprehend the meaning of celibacy in the Christian community, that the multidimensional aspects of the pastoral figure must be understood. The

priest does not stand alone, after all, as the individual summoned to be celibate. He shares this gift with the religious
who also serve the Christian community. There is something appropriate, then, about having the men and women
who are called to be the servants of the Church stand together in celibate dedication at the very heart of the Christian community. One of the gifts they have to give to the
community is the full donation of their manhood and
womanhood through their affirmation of celibacy.

The meaning of celibacy probably cannot be expressed
effectively in the Church by men and women who live totally separate and unrelated lives. Celibacy can and does
make sense if it is perceived as a condition of life for the
priest, brother, and sister who share together the responsibility of bringing the Church to life through vital Christian
communities. If this celibacy is a necessary dimension for
the growth of the Christian community, then it is a means
by which the Spirit brings life to that community. Indeed a
very open and undefended celibacy may be a basic and
essential dynamic for bringing the Church into being under
the action of the Spirit.

Pastoral themes make sense insofar as they bring the
men and women of the Church together, not for the sake
of themselves, but for deepening and strengthening the human foundation for the growth of men and women in relationship around them. The pastoral team provides a living
model because it reflects the masculine and feminine aspects
of the Church as a people. It is, in fact, in the relationship
of a pastoral team which exists for the sake of the Christian
community that the priest and the sister or religious brother

solve their identity crisis. They richly discover the meaning of their lives as they give themselves in order that a community can grow around them in response to the Spirit. This realization of identity arises from human experience more than from theological tracts or encyclicals. So, too, each Christian who enters the community thereby engages himself in the process of achieving his own identity as a Christian. It is for this mature identity in Christ that the members of the community have been prepared by Baptism and Confirmation, those Sacraments of the Spirit which enable their growth in relationship to others in the human condition.

This process of growth in relationship to each other with the pastoral figures as the core of the community's development is not an easy one. These are the essential features of the incarnation which is the first and indispensable stage of the process of growth in the Spirit, Redemptive death occurs as each member must face a community honestly and truthfully just as he or she is. It is one place where masks and facades must gradually be dropped or the community never gets anywhere. This is a very intense and demanding human process. It is one that is aided because of the availability of the persons of the priests and religious who struggle with the membership in a deeply human way as they strive to forge deeper bonds of fidelity with one another.

There are many difficulties that may seem homely at first sight but which are, in fact, aspects of redemptive death. It is possible, for example, for one member of a family to grow at a rate that exceeds that of another member of his own family. A husband may change more quickly or more slowly

religious communities and dioceses away from themselves and toward the ideal of the service of the Church. This is the only way that the provincialism and self-concern that have impeded the fullness of the pastoral presence of the Church in the world can be overcome. There must be a deepened sense of commitment shared across the ranks of all the servants of the Church from the Pope down through all the men and women who gladly give their lives to it. The first loyalty is to the Church, not as a monolithic organization or a conquering world power, but as a saving and indispensable presence in the world. It is time for renewal to let all the arguments about revised schedules and reformed habits fall aside, so that seminarians, priests, and religious can confront the basic issues which must be understood if they are to fulfill their vocations of service. The fundamental issue is to understand the meaning of the Church and its ministry to the human race. Singularly enough, we have given very little time to the discussion of this basic, if difficult, question.

The hour is already late, according to many observers, for the world to begin dealing with the proliferating threats to the human race itself. A recent *Saturday Review* writer quoted scientists Jerome Wiesner and Herbert York on the arms race:

Both sides in the arms race are . . . confronted by the dilemma of steadily increasing military power and steadily decreasing National security. It is our considered professional judgment that this dilemma has no technical solution . . . If the great powers continue to look for solutions in the area of science and technology only, the result will be to worsen the situation.[2]

One must wonder whether churchmen and church-women listen to and understand these cries which choke the throat of mankind. Do they sense that they have a role to play in saving man from the slow strangulation of the technology that has already darkened his skies, polluted his rivers, and can provide no answer to the terrors of a nuclear competition? Is there a more relevant presence for the world to experience than that of the Church whose chief concern is to assist man in finding life, abundant life? If the Church is to respond to these and any of a dozen other current problems from abortion to heart transplants, it will have to present a more flexible and freer pastoral role to its servants. It can no longer dominate or control the lives of priests and religious as it has done in the past. It cannot limit the priestly mode of life or that of professed religious to certain highly stylized forms which may hobble rather than facilitate their participation in the pastoral ministry of the Church.

Religious communities must give up false models of perfection which are the truly irrelevant notions in the world today so that their members can take on the task of relevance in relationship to the questions which keep mankind awake at night. There will be diverse forms, far more freedom of action and diversity in conditions of life, far more self-support and participation in the ordinary economic framework of society, far more commitment to the spirit of the Gospels than to the letter of religious rules and regulations. An openness to this kind of radical change must be maintained if the pastoral presence of the Church in the world is to be more than a shadow or a wispy vision.

The important thing is for the Church to sense its deeply human calling and to accept this invitation to live at that fine point of tension where the secular and the sacred intermingle. It is not merely a question of whether the Church will survive. In fact, the Church will never find the solution to its problems if survival is its only aim. The issue is whether mankind will survive. It is in losing ourselves in response to this question that we will find ourselves as the Church, a truly saving corporate presence in the anguished family of man.

But the time is late and no diocese or religious community which can think only in terms of itself will have any future. Perhaps Robert L. Heilbroner's reflections (also quoted by the above-mentioned *Saturday Review* writer) should be writ large on the walls of all the churches that are supposed to be the shrines of the abiding and saving presence of the Church itself.

The coming generation will be the last generation to seize control over technology before technology has irreversably seized control over it. A generation is not much time, but it is *some* time. . . .[3]

The Church can splendidly renew its life as a pastoral presence in the world in this generation for the sake of the world it is meant to save. A generation is not much time, but it is *some* time. For men and women truly open to the Spirit it is *enough* time.

Notes

1. Sigmund Dragastin, "What's Happened to the Priest's Prestige?", *America*, February 24, 1968, p. 257 and *passim*.
2. Quoted by Wilbur Ferry, "Must We Rewrite the Constitution to Control Technology?" *The Saturday Review*, March 2, 1968, p. 54.
3. Quoted by Wilbur Ferry, *ibid*.